More Sweatshirts With Style

Mary Mulari

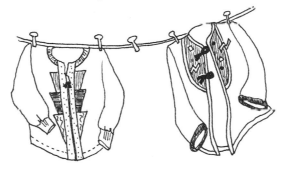

Chilton
BOOK COMPANY
Radnor, Pennsylvania

Published in Radnor, Pennsylvania 19089, by Chilton Book Company

Designed by Lisa J. F. Palmer
Photography by G. W. Tucker Studios (Styling by Mary Mulari)
The following registered trademark terms appear in this book:

Clover 2	Stitch Witchery
Decor Six	Stretch & Sew
Dylon	Styrofoam
Fiskars	Sulky Sliver
Lycra	Ultrasuede
Polarfleece	Velcro
Prym Vario	YLI Pearl Crown Rayon
Rit	

Manufactured in the United States of America

Library of Congress Cataloging-in-Publication Data

Mulari, Mary.
    More sweatshirts with style/Mary Mulari.
        p.   cm
    Includes index.
    ISBN 0–8019–8759–8 (pbk.)
    1. Sweatshirts. 2. Sewing. 3. Applique—Patterns.
    I.Title.
TT649.M83 1996
746.9'2—dc20   96-20440
                                                          CIP

2 3 4 5 6 7 8 9 0   5 4 3 2 1 0 9 8 7

This book is dedicated, with love and appreciation, to Barry for his continuing interest, support, and good humor

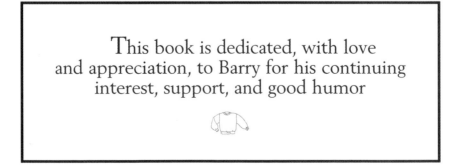

Contents

Preface v

Acknowledgments vi

Introduction 1

Chapter 1. **Getting Started** 2

   ➤ Equipment and Supplies 2

   ➤ Steps That Ensure Success 4

   ➤ Time-Tested Techniques 6

Chapter 2. **Clever Collars and Novel Necklines** 13

   ➤ Zipper Collar 13

   ➤ Cross-Over Ribbing Collar 17

   ➤ Two-Polo Collar Overlapping Neckline 20

   ➤ Funnel Collar with Zipper 21

       Funnel Collar with Buttons 23

       Funnel Collar with Buttons and Shoulder Opening 24

       Funnel Drawstring Collar .27

       Funnel Collar with Woven (Non-Stretch) Fabric 29

   ➤ Two-Piece Polo Collar Neckline 31

   ➤ U Neck with Insert 33

   ➤ Neckline with a Dickey 36

   ➤ Circle Neckline with Running Stitches 38

       Circle Neckline with Fabric Insert 40

Chapter 3. **Classic Cardigans** 43

   ➤ Zip-Front Cardigan 43

   ➤ Banded Cardigan with Matching Ribbing 48

   ➤ Banded Cardigan with Contrast Ribbing 52

Chapter 4. **Creative Cuffs, Sleeves, Pockets, and Hems** 56

   ➤ Replacement Sleeve Cuffs 56

   ➤ Two-Piece Cuffs 57

   ➤ Sleeve-Gathering Trim 59

   ➤ Zippered Sleeve Pockets 61

   ➤ Hem Facing with Shirt Tails .64

➤ Tunic Extension with Zipper 66

     Two-Piece Tunic Extension 68

➤ Hidden Side Pocket with Triangle Ends 70

Chapter 5. Applique Additions 73

➤ The Basics of Satin Stitch Applique 73

➤ Dimensional Applique with Tulle 75

➤ Scrub Stitch Applique 79

➤ Scissor Cuttings Applique 81

Chapter 6. Other Decorating Strategies 84

➤ Large-Collar Mock Front 84

➤ Mock Front Cardigan with Dickey Insert 87

➤ Mock Front Placket with Toggle Closures 90

➤ Nordic Sweatshirt 93

➤ Easy-Lace Buttonhole Trim 96

➤ Fleece-Woven Front 99

➤ Relaxed Weaving 102

➤ Cool and Unusual Stripes 105

➤ Sponge Painting and Stitching .108

➤ Mitten Gallery 111

Chapter 7. Readers' Gallery of Sweatshirt Ideas 116

➤ Buttons and Bows Sweatshirt by Marilyn Gatz 116

➤ Elegant Beaded Sweatershirt by Nancy Bednar 119

➤ Flatlock Frenzy by Jenny Osborn 122

➤ Some Bunny Sweatshirt by Janis Giblin 125

➤ Life's a Party Sweatshirt by Kelly Harlow 127

➤ Trio of Trillium by Barb Prihoda 130

➤ Shaped-Up Sweatshirt by Steph Barry 136

➤ From the Wilds of Canada by Jan Saunders 141

Cabin/Trees Applique Pattern 146

Resources 147

Behind the Readers' Gallery 148

Bibliography 150

Index 151

About the Author 154

Preface

During one of the most marvelous summers ever in northern Minnesota, you would have found me indoors preparing this book, sewing sweatshirts and writing the instructions after sewing.

I started the projects by prewashing piles of shirts and fabrics and then sat down to sew up my new ideas. My first idea was a jacket-style sweatshirt. I was so excited to try it because in my mind it was going to be a dynamite project. It was a flop. So, I turned to a new collar idea and sewed it in two versions, but you won't find that one in the book either. I was off to a discouraging start with my book.

But then, I sewed the Nordic Sweatshirt, found the pewter clasps for the neckline closure, and bingo! That was the first of many successful projects—thank goodness!

For me, sewing and writing a book means solitary confinement in my sewing parlour and at the computer. (After I found the "sewing parlour" sign at the Blueberry Festival in Ely, I renamed my sewing room.) I surfaced into civilization early every weekday morning to join my walking group on our 3-mile hike around Aurora, with the coffee stop at Hank's Bar & Grill. That was a dose of fresh summer air and the unique perspective and conversations of the Sunset Walkie-Talkies. For a response to my sweatshirt projects, I had the Honesty Committee—Nancy, Kathy, and my sister Sarah. They all raved about the Nordic Sweatshirt too.

When it came time to transfer my sewing notes to the computer, I took my papers and laptop computer out on the screened deck. (Most summers, the screen is necessary so you don't become a human mosquito banquet. This particular summer, we didn't get many, which added to the quality of the season.) As my friend Marty would say, it was a little slice of heaven to be outdoors in the sunshine with a quiet breeze and the green woods to set the scene. I made sure to follow the advice on a wonderful answering machine message I heard early in the summer: "Take a moment to appreciate this day."

Additional sustenance came from Barry's large and bountiful vegetable garden and the music of Bill Staines, Claudia Schmidt, and Sally Rogers, and Minnesota Public Radio. I also took time to enjoy the petunias in the window boxes and decided I'll try impatiens next year so I won't be a slave to picking off dead blossoms.

And so this book is done and it's a great relief. A beautiful summer has turned into a wonderful autumn—so far. Wherever you are, join me as I follow the answering machine advice: "Take a moment to appreciate this day." And, have fun using the ideas in this book.

Mary Mulari
September 1995
Aurora, MN

Acknowledgments

Thanks to many companies and individuals, I am able to sew and write here in the North Woods of Minnesota. I have had the support of many people who have believed in me and my work, and it's only right to begin this book acknowledging their contributions. Though I write and sew alone in my office and sewing parlour, I feel their support and encouragement, and this is the time to say that I could never do my work without their help.

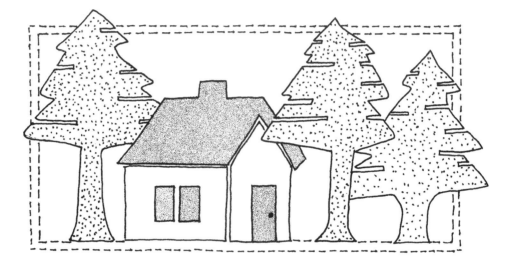

Companies that have generously assisted with machines, materials, and knowledge include Bernina of America, Elna Inc., Fiskars, Gutermann Threads, Handler Textile Corp., Kunin Felt, New Home Janome Sewing Machine Co., C.M. Offray & Sons, P & B Textiles, Pfaff American Sales Corp., Stretch and Sew Patterns, Sulky of America, Therm O Web, Viking Sewing Machine Co., VIP Fabrics, and Wimpole Street Creations.

Sewing friends who share ideas and always show interest in my work include Gail Brown, Margaret Croswell, Rita Farro, Nancy Harp, and Nancy Zieman.

The eight contributors to the Readers' Gallery generously shared their sweatshirts and instructions. I value their additions to this book and appreciate their cooperation. My thanks to Steph Barry, Nancy Bednar, Marilyn Gatz, Janis Giblin, Kelly Harlow, Jenny Osborn, Barb Prihoda, and Jan Saunders.

Thanks to Chilton Book Company and the efforts of Stacey Follin, Susan Keller, and Robbie Fanning, who improve my books with their editing and smart ideas.

Then there are the people who love my books even though they don't sew: my husband, my sisters and brother, my parents, my college roommates, and many others who I know will always be interested, ask questions, and want every book.

The enthusiastic reception to my first Chilton book, *Sweatshirts with Style,* led me to write this second book about improvements to the garment everyone loves.

I feel very lucky to be able to thank so many people.

Introduction

Welcome to my new collection of ways to alter and trim sweatshirts. This book is a follow-up to my first Chilton title, *Sweatshirts with Style*, and it offers all-new ways to change and improve everyone's "comfort" garment, the sweatshirt.

Since I've been working with them, the reputation of sweatshirts has changed from lowly, insignificant gymnasium wear to desirable and stylish clothing for every day. We've grown to love the comfort of sweatshirt fleece and now, thanks to easy sewing techniques, the changes and decorations that add personality and flair.

This book offers alterations, decorations, and appliques for you to mix and match on sweatshirts. In the color photos, you will see how I combined different project ideas; follow my examples, or try your own combinations. What's more, think of the word "sweatshirt" as a symbol for any plain garment you can make better with your sewing skills and the instructions in this book—and use the alterations and trims on other clothes too.

Due to the popularity of many of the projects in *Sweatshirts with Style*, I developed additional ideas in the same categories for this book. You'll find more cardigan alteration ideas in chapter 4, along with several new mock fronts (chapter 8) in the style of the very popular nautical shirt from *Sweatshirts with Style*.

Be sure to read chapter 1 before beginning any of the projects. It will give you an overview of the equipment and supplies you'll need to complete these projects as well as the basic techniques you'll find yourself using over and over again.

As you work with this book, add notes in the margins and the blank areas. Use my instructions and suggestions as starting points, then try your own innovations. I hope my ideas will inspire you to approach these projects in new and different ways and add your own innovations, making your sweatshirts true "designer originals."

Write to me with your sweatshirt creations, questions, and suggestions. I enjoy hearing from you. My address is Box 87-C3, Aurora, MN 55705.

Have fun reading about and sewing more sweatshirts with style.

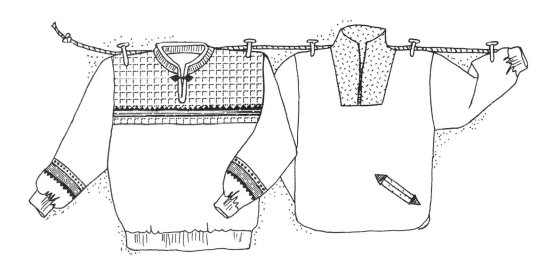

1

Getting Started

Equipment and Supplies

To work on any of the sweatshirt projects in this book, you will need certain basic equipment and supplies. Many of the items listed in this section are already in your sewing room, but it's a good idea to check for them, making sure you have enough on hand (Fig. 1).

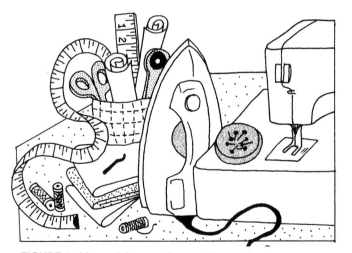

FIGURE 1. Many of the supplies you'll need for these projects are already in your sewing room.

Sewing Machine and Serger

The main piece of equipment is your sewing machine. It should be in good working order, cleaned, and oiled, if necessary. While you do not need the most deluxe machine to complete these sweatshirt pro-jects, a newer machine will help you do techniques like traditional satin stitch applique more smoothly.

If you have a serger, it will also be useful. Keep it near your sewing machine so it's convenient to use.

Iron

The other piece of equipment to keep nearby and to use frequently is the iron. As most sewing teachers will emphasize, pressing each seam after it is sewn is the best advice and helps you avoid the "loving hands at home" look to your sewing. The advice applies to sweatshirt sewing as well as tailoring.

Sewing Equipment

You will use the supplies in your sewing basket—pins, scissors, seam ripper, tape measure, 6" (15cm) ruler, chalk marker and washable marking pen, rotary cutter and mat, yardstick, hand sewing needles, and so on—for many of the projects in this book. Pinking shears will help you trim and clip seam allowances all in one easy step; liquid seam sealant will provide a fast, permanent way to prevent raveling on serged seams and other areas.

Fabric and Thread

You'll need a variety of fabrics for these sweatshirt projects. Feel free to use the fabric of your choice, unless the directions specify otherwise. While many of us have a well-supplied stash to browse through (That's a Minnesota-style understatement!), some projects will lead you to the fabric store for just the perfect fabric, so you'll be able to add to your stash.

Also, make sure that the thread matches the fabrics and/or sweatshirt color for the project, unless otherwise specified. It's a funny thing about thread—when it matches well you don't notice it, but when it doesn't, it jumps right out at you.

Interfacing

For the sweatshirt projects requiring interfacing, a light-weight fusible variety will be your best choice to avoid stiffening the sweatshirt. My favorite interfacing is the tricot knit fusible interfacing that works so well to stabilize fabric but doesn't make it feel like a board. When you think about it, we like sweatshirts because their fabric is soft and it gives. The same two qualities are found in tricot knit fusible interfacing.

Paper-Backed Fusible Web and Stabilizers

Both paper-backed fusible web and stabilizers are crucial to smooth stitching on many of the sweatshirt projects, so it's good to get accustomed to using them.

There are many brands of paper-backed fusible web in different weights for sewing. Try several of them for applique and other projects and experiment to see which ones you prefer. Also, be sure to read the instructions that accompany the paper-backed fusible web regarding iron temperature and length of fusing.

There are also several different types of stabilizers, ranging from pin-on and tear-away varieties to liquid and water-soluble and rinse-away varieties. Work with these as well to find your favorite types and have them on hand so they're easy to use and there when you need them. Keep in mind: They are especially important when sewing against the grain.

Sweatshirts

For any of the projects in this book, you can either purchase ready-to-wear sweatshirts or make your own. With fleece fabric and matching ribbing available at sewing stores and through mail-order sources, it is easy to sew or serge a sweatshirt from scratch. However, any sweatshirt you alter or decorate should be brand new, so that it has plenty of wear left in it and continues to look good after many more launderings.

Prewash all sweatshirts before decorating them. Turn the shirt inside out any time it is laundered to protect the right side of the fabric. Also prewash the fabrics that you'll use to decorate the shirt. I recommend that you also prewash and air dry the lightweight fusible interfacing used in many of the projects. Of course, limiting the time that sweatshirts and fabrics circulate in a hot clothes dryer is also a good idea. My suggestion: Place sweatshirts in the dryer for a few minutes to bounce out the wrinkles, then hang them out to air dry.

For each shirt you trim to give as a gift or sell, add a label with instructions on how to take care of the sweatshirt. Use my example or write your own suggestions for maintaining the life and good looks of your creations (Fig. 2).

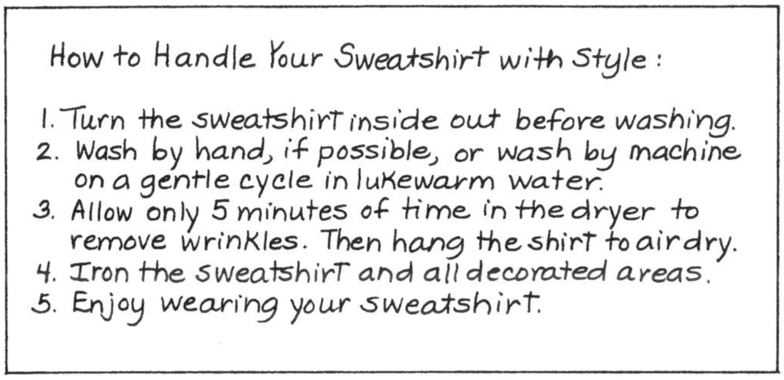

How to Handle Your Sweatshirt with Style :

1. Turn the sweatshirt inside out before washing.
2. Wash by hand, if possible, or wash by machine on a gentle cycle in lukewarm water.
3. Allow only 5 minutes of time in the dryer to remove wrinkles. Then hang the shirt to air dry.
4. Iron the sweatshirt and all decorated areas.
5. Enjoy wearing your sweatshirt.

FIGURE 2. Tags like this one will help others take care of your special creations.

Now that you have the basic equipment and supplies, take time to review the following basic procedures, many of which you will use to create the stylish sweatshirts in this book.

Steps That Ensure Success

This section could also be called Steps That Should Not Be Skipped. If you are altering or decorating a sweatshirt, you'll need to know how the shirt fits you and where you'd like the decorations to appear. Planning symmetrical decorations requires finding the center front of the shirt. My foolproof procedure will help you make sure that you're properly "centered." Finally, if you have both a serger and a sewing machine, you'll want to read my suggestions for when to use which machine.

Always, Always Try on the Sweatshirt First

Trying on the sweatshirt is an important step in all of these sweatshirt projects. It enables you to check the overall fit, make design plans—and create a stylish and professional-looking sweatshirt.

1 Check the fit of the shirt, its neckline, and its sleeve and bottom lengths.

2 Mark the bustline points with pins, a chalk marker, or a washable marking pen. These marks will help you determine where to place your de-

signs and help you avoid the "bra syndrome"—having two large, prominent designs directly on the bustline (Fig. 3). Remember: People will inevitably look at the areas you decorate.

3 Mark the ends of your shoulders and any other features you need to remember as you plan the shirt alteration or designs (Fig. 4).

FIGURE 3. Something to avoid: a sweatshirt trimmed with two prominent designs directly on the bustline.

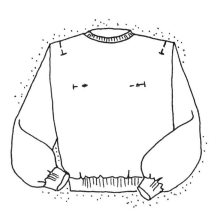

FIGURE 4. Try on the shirt and mark the bustline and shoulder ends with pins.

There will be many reminders in this book to try on the sweatshirt to test various alterations. Like the carpenter's law "Measure twice, cut once," you'll save yourself time, frustration, and ripping if you take the time to try on the shirt *before* cutting or sewing.

Don't Be Fooled: Find the Real Center Front of Your Sweatshirt

On a purchased sweatshirt, it's very tempting to assume that the faint fold line on the front is the center front line. Sometimes it is, but double-check it. This is a very important step, especially for making cardigans and other alterations where an accurate center front line is crucial. Also, look for the tag at the back of the sweatshirt neckline to ensure that you are marking and working on the front of the sweatshirt. (Ask me why I remind you to do this!)

1 Press the sides of the sweatshirt to set a crease, so you can accurately meet the two side lines of the shirt at the bottom edges and pin them together (Fig. 5).

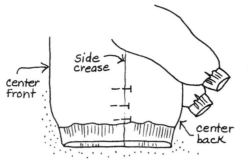

FIGURE 5. Press to form lines on the sweatshirt sides and then pin the two lines together.

2 Meet either the raglan or shoulder seams and pin the sweatshirt together on those seams (Fig. 6).

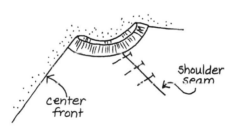

FIGURE 6. Pin the shoulder seams together to form a fold at the shirt center front.

3 With the neckline and the bottom edges pinned in half, the center front line of the shirt will form along the fold. Press the fold carefully, and re-move the pins. For a longer-lasting line, draw on the foldline with a chalk marker or a washable marking pen.

Deciding When to Sew and/or Serge

The project instructions in this book will often say "sew" or "sew or serge." In most cases, either technique will work. You do not need a serger for most of the sweatshirt projects, but if you have one and are familiar with it, use it in tandem with your sewing machine to give your seams a more polished look.

1 If you're uncertain about a technique you're working on or the fit of a piece you're adding, sew first with a longer stitch length, so you can remove it easily, if necessary. Remember: Serged stitching is more difficult to remove if you make a mistake or change your mind, and the seam allowances for these projects are generally only ¼" (6mm) wide, so there isn't much excess fabric to play with.

2 After sewing, you can follow up by serging over the seam to cover the fabric edges with thread. A serged finish looks especially nice on the inside of the neckline.

Time-Tested Techniques

This is an important section of the book. These time-tested instructions and recommendations are based on lots of experience working with sweatshirts. They are meant to help you save time and produce sweatshirts that are both stylish and professional looking. The techniques explained in this section are required for many of the sweatshirt projects in this book, so I gathered them here in the first chapter for easy reference. Putting them all in one place, rather than discussing each one every time it is used, helped me save space and include even more sweatshirt ideas for you.

Reading through these instructions before you begin working on actual sweatshirts will help you understand many of the procedures used in the book. Once you've tried the techniques a few times, you will be able to complete your sweatshirts without referring back to this section.

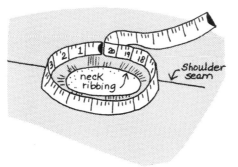

FIGURE 7. Measure around the neckline with the tape measure on its edge rather than flat.

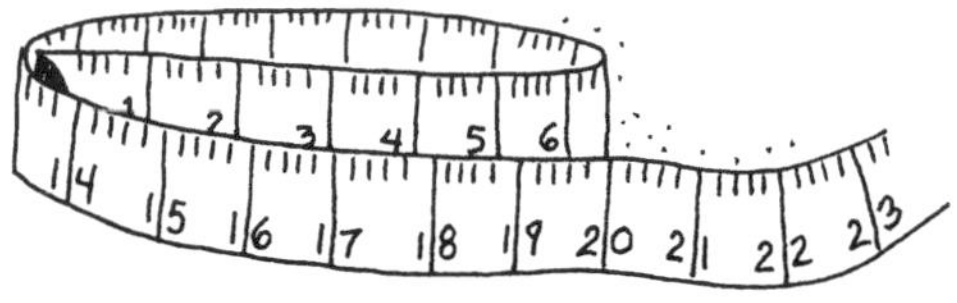

FIGURE 8. To find ⅔ of a measurement, fold the tape measure in thirds.

Measuring around the Neckline with a Tape Measure

Many times, you will be asked to measure the distance around a sweatshirt neckline. If you use the tape measure flat and try to swivel it around the neck, your measurement will not be accurate. Instead, try the following technique:

1 Use the tape measure on its edge to measure the neckline. It will definitely be easier and more precise (Fig. 7).

2 The next instruction will often require that you calculate ⅔ or ¾ of the measurement to make the new collar piece or neck treatment. In case you are not a math whiz (join the crowd!) you can use the tape measure to make a fast calculation. If the neck measurement is 20″ (51cm), fold the tape measure in thirds, and the numbers on the tape will tell you that ⅔ of 20″ (51cm) is 13⅜″ (34cm) (Fig. 8). If the neck measurement is 20″ (51cm), fold the tape measure in fourths, and the numbers on the tape will tell you that ¾ of 20″ (51cm) is 15″ (38cm).

➤ **Sew-er's Note:** While a calculator will tell you that ⅔ of 20″ (51cm) actually equals 13⅓″ (34cm), when working with a tape measure, it's easier to find the ⅜ mark than the ⅓ mark.

Staystitching the Neckline <u>before</u> Removing the Ribbing

For most neckline alterations you'll be asked to staystitch around the neckline, close to the neckline seam, before removing the original neck ribbing. This precautionary stitching will save the neckline from stretching out of shape and will also keep the shoulder or raglan seams from opening after the ribbing is removed.

1 Select thread to match the sweatshirt color so the staystitching is hidden, and use a standard stitch length or a shorter stitch length.

2 Sew very close to the neckline seam, stitching *inside* the shirt, on the wrong side of the fabric. Move the needle position on the sewing machine to the right, close to the stitching that holds the ribbing to the shirt (Fig. 9). If the project directions suggest stitching ½" (1.3cm) from the ribbing for a larger neck opening, draw marks and/or a continuous line ½" (1.3cm) from the ribbing around the neckline before staystitching (Fig. 10).

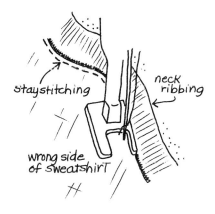

FIGURE 9. Staystitch around the neckline before removing the ribbing. Stitch on the wrong side of the neckline as close to the ribbing edge as possible.

FIGURE 10. Mark ½" from the ribbing all the way around the neck to locate the staystitching line.

3 Cut off the original neckline or neck ribbing.

STAYSTITCHING OTHER SWEATSHIRT AREAS

Besides asking you to staystitch the neckline, some projects will ask that you staystitch on each side of the shirt's center front line to stabilize the fabric before cutting it open to make a cardigan (Fig. 11).

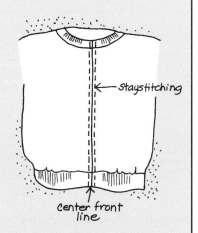

FIGURE 11. Staystitch on each side of the sweatshirt front line before cutting open the shirt for a cardigan front.

I have not found it necessary to staystitch before removing the cuffs or bottom ribbing, but feel free to staystitch these areas as well.

Removing Ribbing

There is more than one way to remove ribbing from a sweatshirt: (1) Staystitch around the ribbing, unless you are working on the bottom of the sweatshirt or the cuffs, in which case you can skip this step. Cut off the seam allowances and threads holding the ribbing to the shirt (Fig. 12). (2) Cut the threads that attach the ribbing to the shirt. Because I like to preserve the actual shirt neckline, ribbing edges, and other edges of the shirt, I prefer and recommend that you follow the second method and use a seam ripper to cut the threads (Fig. 13).

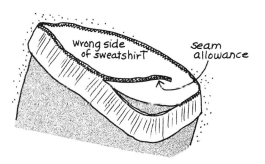

FIGURE 12. One way to remove the ribbing: Cut off the seam allowance and stitching connecting the ribbing to the shirt.

FIGURE 13. Surgical seam ripper.

1 Hold the seam ripper vertically and use it like a saw. Insert it into the "ditch" and while holding onto the shirt behind the ripper, work the ripper up and down, cutting the threads (Fig. 14). This method saves you from picking out many tiny thread ends because the threads can be pulled off as long pieces, and when the shirt and ribbing are separated, the cut edges will be the same as when the shirt was made at the factory.

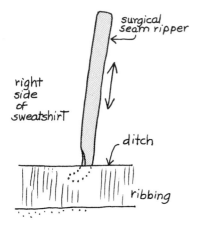

FIGURE 14. With the seam ripper inserted in the ditch, use a sawing motion up and down, with the sharp edge cutting the threads holding the ribbing to the shirt.

2 Save the ribbing. Sometimes when you remove ribbing you re-use it on another part of the sweatshirt. However, even if you do not plan to use it, save it for another sweatshirt project. You'll find that a stash of extra ribbing will come in handy.

Marking Quarter Portions of the Neckline

Use this technique for marking quarter portions of the neckline and fitting edges of the sweatshirt together with ribbing or other fabrics for collars or facings.

1 Meet the shoulder or raglan seams of the neckline together and fold the shirt's neckline in half with folds at center front and center back (Fig. 15). For hemline or sleeve edges, bring the sides together to create a fold at center front and back (Fig. 16).

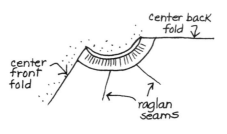

FIGURE 15. Fold the shirt at center front and back and meet the raglan or shoulder seams.

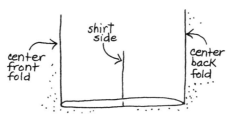

FIGURE 16. Match the lines for the shirt sides to create a fold at the shirt's center front and back.

2 Mark the center front and back with pins, a chalk marker, or a washable marking pen. Then fold the shirt again by bringing the center front and back locations together. The folds created are the halfway points between the front and back; mark the folds (Fig. 17).

Remember that on a sweatshirt with set-in sleeves, the midway points will *not* be on the shoulder seams.

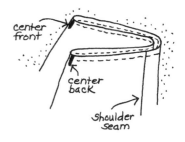

FIGURE 17. Match the center front and back marks and fold to find the halfway points between centers. This will determine the location of the quarter portion marks.

3 Now do the same quarter portion folding and marking on the collar, ribbing, or facing fabric that will be sewn to the shirt (Fig. 18).

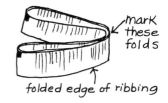

FIGURE 18. Mark quarter portions on ribbing or collars.

4 With the right side of the collar or other fabric facing the right side of the sweatshirt, pin the two layers together, first by matching the quarter portions on each fabric and then by adjusting and pinning between (Fig. 19). Ribbing and knit fabrics will stretch easily to fit the garment fabric.

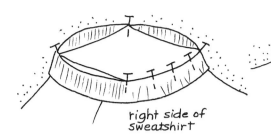

FIGURE 19. Match and pin together the quarter portion marks on ribbing and sweatshirt. Add extra pins between the quarter points to hold the fabrics together.

FIGURE 21. Ribbing seam offset in back neckline.

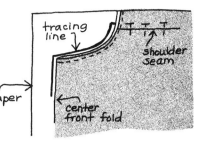

FIGURE 22. Trace the neck outline from the center front to ¼″ past the shoulder line.

5 Sew or serge the fabric, collar, or facing to the sweatshirt.

Positioning the New Collar Seam in the Neckline

There is a difference of opinion on where in the neckline to place the new collar seam. Some of us automatically position the seamline at center back, using that point as one of the quarter portion marks (Fig. 20). Ready-to-wear garments also feature this seam placement. Others believe that a center back seam placement betrays a home-sewn garment and move the seamline closer to the shoulder seam so it's less obvious (Fig. 21). Either way is acceptable. Go with your best instincts.

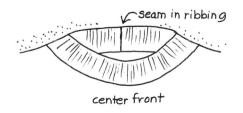

FIGURE 20. Ribbing seam placed at center back neckline.

Making Facings

For several of the sweatshirt alterations, you will need facings to finish the new necklines and the new bottom edges of the cuffs and shirts.

Facings for Necklines

After experimenting, I have found that two-piece neck facings work best in sweatshirt necklines.

1 Staystitch around the shirt's neckline and cut off the ribbing, using the instructions on pages 6–7.

2 Fold the shirt neckline in half, meet the shoulder or raglan seams, and pin them together.

3 On paper, trace the front neckline edge from the center front fold edge to the shoulder line, adding an extra ¼″ (6mm) beyond the shoulder line (Fig. 22). On a second piece of paper, trace the back neckline in the same way, also adding ¼″ (6mm) at the shoulder line (Fig. 23).

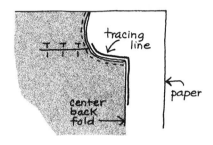

FIGURE 23. Place the sweatshirt folded back neckline on paper and trace the outline, extending the line ¼″ past the shoulder.

4 On the paper patterns, measure 3″ (7.5cm) from the neckline edges to draw the outside edge of the facings. On the back facing, you might want to extend the center back to 5″ (12.5cm) to duplicate ready-to-wear facings that are longer in the back than the front (Fig. 24).

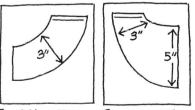

Front Neck Facing   Back Neck Facing

FIGURE 24. Draw the front and back facings 3″ wide, or extend the center back facing to 5″.

5 Place the two facing patterns on folded fabric and cut out each one (Fig. 25). Also cut out two facings from lightweight fusible interfacing, such as tricot knit fusible interfacing. Fuse the interfacing pieces to the wrong sides of the fabric facings.

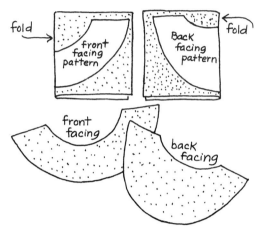

FIGURE 25. Cut the front and back facings from folded fabric.

6 Sew the two facing pieces together at the shoulder lines, positioning the right sides of fabric together and using a ¼" (6mm) seam allowance (Fig. 26).

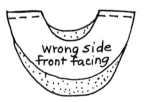

FIGURE 26. Sew the two facings together at the shoulders.

7 Press the seams. Zigzag or serge the outside edge of the facing (Fig. 27). Now the

facing is ready to be sewn to the sweatshirt's neckline.

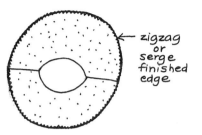

FIGURE 27. Finish the outer edge of the facing by zigzag stitching or serging.

Facings for Cuffs and Bottom Edges

Unlike sweatshirt necklines, cuffs and bottom edges are straight, so it is easier to make facings for them.

Simply place the shirt edges on folded fabric, or measure the edges and cut out strips of fabric for the facings. The strips should be 3" (7.5cm) wide and as long as needed to go around the cuffs or bottom edge, adding ¼" (6mm) for seam allowances (Fig. 28). You can also apply lightweight fusible interfacing for extra stability.

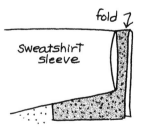

FIGURE 28. To make the sleeve end facings, place the sleeves on folded fabric and cut fabric bands, allowing for seam allowances where the facings will be sewn together.

Understitching the New Neckline or Collar

After sewing or serging a new collar or edge facing on the sweatshirt, I recommend following with a row of understitching, which also looks like topstitching, to sew the seam allowances to the sweatshirt. This stitching detail creates the flatter, neater-looking necklines that you find on store-bought clothing (Fig. 29).

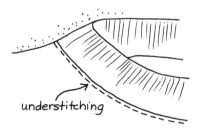

FIGURE 29. Understitch to secure the seam allowances to the sweatshirt.

1 After sewing, press the neckline flat. If there is puckering on the sweatshirt and the seam allowances are stretched out, clip the seam allowances around the neck (Fig. 30).

FIGURE 30. Clip the seam allowance to prevent the seam from puckering.

2 Pin the seam allowances onto the shirt and try the shirt on to check the fit of the neckline. Then, sew around the neckline, approximately ⅛" (3mm) from the "ditch" (Fig. 31). I recommend lengthening the stitch to 3.5 and also sewing slowly and carefully. This stitching line will be very noticeable at the shirt's neckline, especially if it is uneven and carelessly stitched.

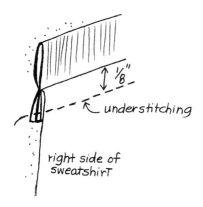

FIGURE 31. To understitch, sew on the right side of the fabric to hold the seam allowance to the garment.

Covering the Back Neck Seam Allowances

I'll agree, sometimes the seam inside the shirt's back neckline looks untidy, especially if you haven't serged the edge or if you have serged it with thread that doesn't match or blend with the color of the shirt. Here's a way to fix the appearance of the inside of the neck, especially from shoulder seam to shoulder seam. It's a trick I learned from studying ready-to-wear clothing.

1 Cut a piece of bias tape the length of the seam allowances between the shoulder seams of the shirt. Pin the bias tape over the seam allowances and sew both edges to the sweatshirt (Fig. 32).

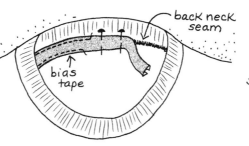

FIGURE 32. Sew bias tape over the back neck seam to cover the seamline and duplicate a detail from ready-to-wear clothing.

2 Match the top thread to the bias tape, and the bobbin thread to the sweatshirt. If you use a sewing machine, two seams will show on the outside of the shirt; if you sew the bias on by hand, no seams will show.

At the same time, sew in your designer label at the back of the neck. It's important to "sign" your art-wear.

Adding a Nifty Zipper with Hidden Seams

Several of the projects use this easy and neat-looking zipper application.

1 Pin and sew (with the zipper foot on the sewing machine) one edge of the zipper along the outside fabric edge

(Fig. 33). Turn back the top ends of the zipper. Sew the other side of the zipper to the opposite side of the collar or facing (Fig. 34)

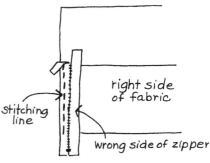

FIGURE 33. Sew one side of the zipper (right side of zipper facing right side of fabric) to the outside edge of the fabric.

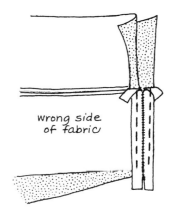

FIGURE 34. Sew the other side of the zipper to the right side of the fabric.

2 Open the zipper (Fig. 35). Bring the back side of the lining over the top of the zipper (Fig. 36). The seam or fold line of the collar or facing will be exposed at the top. Pin the side edge of the lining fabric over the stitched edge of the zipper. Do this on both sides of the zipper. Flip the fabrics over so you can see the previous stitching line and sew along it to attach the lining (Fig. 37).

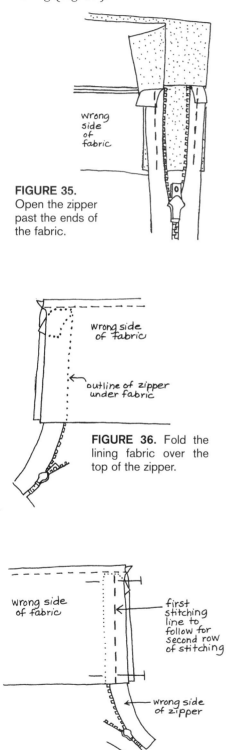

FIGURE 35. Open the zipper past the ends of the fabric.

FIGURE 36. Fold the lining fabric over the top of the zipper.

FIGURE 37. Sew along the first stitching line to attach the back or lining fabric to the zipper.

3 Turn the fabrics right side out and check the zipper. If the top ends are too bulky, turn back to the wrong sides of the collar and trim away excess fabric and zipper tape.

4 On the front side of the zipper, sew across the zipper at the bottom end of the collar or facing and then cut away the excess zipper below the stitching (Fig. 38).

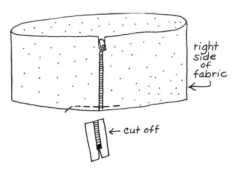

FIGURE 38. Sew across the end of the zipper and then cut off any extra zipper length below the stitching.

Checking and Fixing the Sweatshirt Bottom Edge After Removing the Ribbing

When you remove the bottom ribbing of a sweatshirt, the bottom edge usually requires attention.

1 After you take the ribbing off the bottom of the sweatshirt, press the bottom edge to flatten and smooth out the cut edges. At this time, you may be surprised to find an irregular edge that needs to be straightened before you add a facing or tunic bottom (Fig. 39).

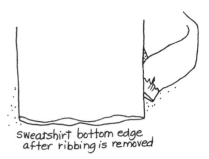

FIGURE 39. You may find an irregular bottom edge on a sweatshirt after the ribbing is removed.

2 Measure down from the sleeve seam to the bottom of the shirt on both sides. If one side is 13" (33cm) long and the other is 13½" 34.5cm), mark the 13" (33cm) point on both sides and draw a straight line across, using a long ruler or yardstick (Fig. 40). Next, cut off the excess fabric to make a straight bottom across the sweatshirt and proceed with the styling change you've chosen.

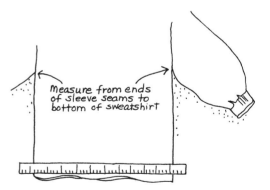

FIGURE 40. Use a ruler or yardstick to draw a line across the sweatshirt to make a new straight bottom edge.

Now that we have the "basics" out of the way, let's start restyling sweatshirts.

2 Clever Collars & Novel Necklines

✦ ZIPPER COLLAR ✦

One thing I like to note about the Zipper Collar shirt is that it's versatile: You can open the zipper and fold back the collar or zip up to give a tall turtleneck effect (Fig. 1).

Change and replace a plain sweatshirt neckline with a new zippered collar. I selected two different fabrics for my inside and outside collars, along with a contrasting black zipper. I made a zipper pull from a strip of Ultrasuede to trim the zipper and make it easier to open and close. I also placed an additional strip of bias fabric over the back seamline to cover the stitching and the raw edges of the collar pieces. (Outer collar and background fabrics are from VIP Fabrics.)

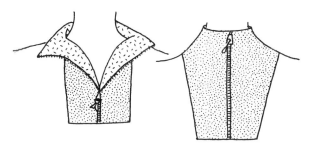

FIGURE 1. Wear the zipper collar open or closed for two different neckline effects.

Supplies Needed

- one sweatshirt
- ½ yd. (46cm) woven or knit fabric for collar (½ yd. of a second fabric if you prefer a different fabric for lining)
- ½ yd. (46cm) lightweight fusible interfacing (optional)
- 9″ (23cm) or 12″ (30.5cm) zipper, or longer
- 15″ (38cm) bias tape (optional)

1 Trace the Zipper Collar Pattern on page 16 onto a piece of paper, and cut it out. Note the grainline instruction and the adjustable foldline notation. Note that the top and bottom edges can be lengthened or shortened, depending on the size of collar you prefer. To check the size of the pattern, cut the collar from scrap fabric and try it on the shirt before cutting out the actual collar pieces.

2 Measure the back of the sweatshirt neckline between the shoulders, using the technique on page 6 and measuring at the bottom edge of the neck ribbing (Fig. 2).

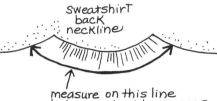

FIGURE 2. Measure the back sweatshirt neckline on the bottom edge of the neck ribbing between the shoulder seams.

3 Add 1″ (2.5cm) to the measurement and divide by 2. Here's an example: The total measure of my sweatshirt neck between the shoulders is 9″ (23cm), so I add 1″ to make it 10″ (25.5cm) and divide that by 2 to get 5″ (12.5cm). Use this measure as the distance to place the notch on the curved edge of the pattern from the fold of the collar fabric (Fig. 3).

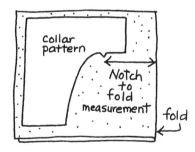

FIGURE 3. Place the collar pattern on folded fabric, placing the notch according to the neckline measurement calculated in steps 2 and 3.

4 Cut two collar pieces. They can be made of the same fabric, but I think it's fun to use two coordinating fabrics. Depending on the fabrics you select for the collar, you may want to interface one collar fabric with lightweight fusible interfacing.

5 Sew or serge the two collar pieces together along the top edge, placing right sides of the fabric together and using a ¼″ (6mm) seam allowance (Fig. 4). Press the seam. For a flatter, neater-looking neckline, understitch the seam allowance to either the outer collar fabric or the collar lining using the instructions on pages 10–11.

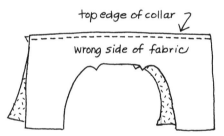

FIGURE 4. With right sides of the fabric together, sew the two collar fabrics together along the top edge of the collar.

6 Next sew the zipper to the collar edges, using the instructions on pages 11–12.

7 Turn both layers under ¼″ (6mm) and press the raw edges at the bottom of the collar. On the curved edges, clip into the seam allowance if you have difficulty turning under the edges (Fig. 5).

FIGURE 5. Turn under and press ¼" around the entire bottom edge of the collar. Clip the curved edges.

8 Using a chalk marker or a washable marking pen, mark the sweatshirt's center back and center front, extending the center front line down the shirt front, as explained on page 5. On the front, also draw a straight perpendicular line 7" (18cm) from the bottom of the neckline ribbing and across center front to help you line up the front edge of the collar (Fig. 6). Mark the center back on the collar.

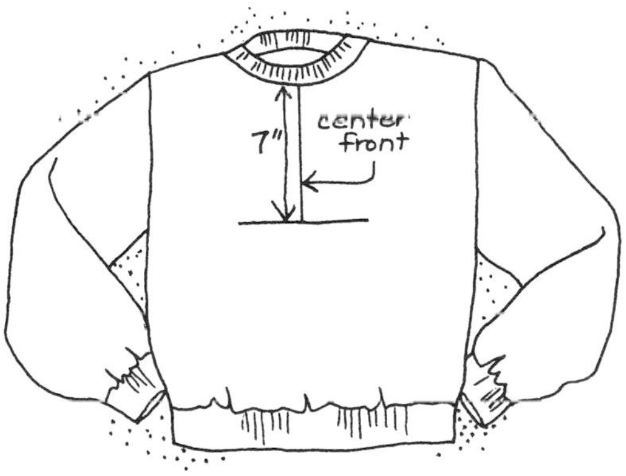

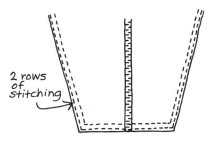

FIGURE 6. Draw a horizontal line across the center front to guide you in centering the collar unit.

9 Begin pinning the collar to the shirt at the center back, over and right below the

bottom of the neck ribbing. The underside of the collar covers the topside of the sweatshirt. Match the notches on the collar to the shoulder seams (Fig. 7). The turned-under edge of the collar will be pinned on below the neck ribbing. Expect to use plenty of pins to secure the collar before sewing.

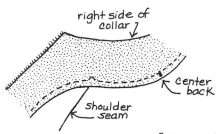

FIGURE 7. Place and pin the collar to the sweatshirt, beginning at center back below the neck ribbing. Align the notches with the shoulder seams.

10 Next, line up and pin the center front of the collar to the center front of the shirt. Attach the remaining collar edges with pins (Fig. 8).

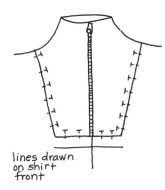

FIGURE 8. Pin the collar unit to the sweatshirt front, using the guide lines drawn on the shirt to place the collar straight on the shirt.

11 Sew the collar to the shirt, sewing close to the folded-under collar edge and then sew a second row of stitching ⅛" (3mm) from the first row (Fig. 9).

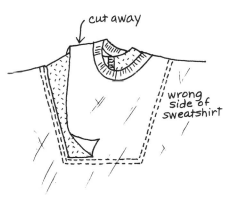

FIGURE 9. Sew two rows of stitching around the bottom edge of the collar unit.

12 Turn the shirt inside out and cut away the sweatshirt neckline and fleece inside the stitching line (Fig. 10).

FIGURE 10. On the wrong side of the sweatshirt, cut away the shirt neckline inside the stitching line for the zipper collar attachment.

13 Try on the shirt—it's ready to wear! Zip up the collar on a windy day for neck warmth, or open the collar on a warmer day to cool off. If you'd like to neaten the back seam allowance inside the shirt's neckline, cover it with bias tape using the technique on page 11.

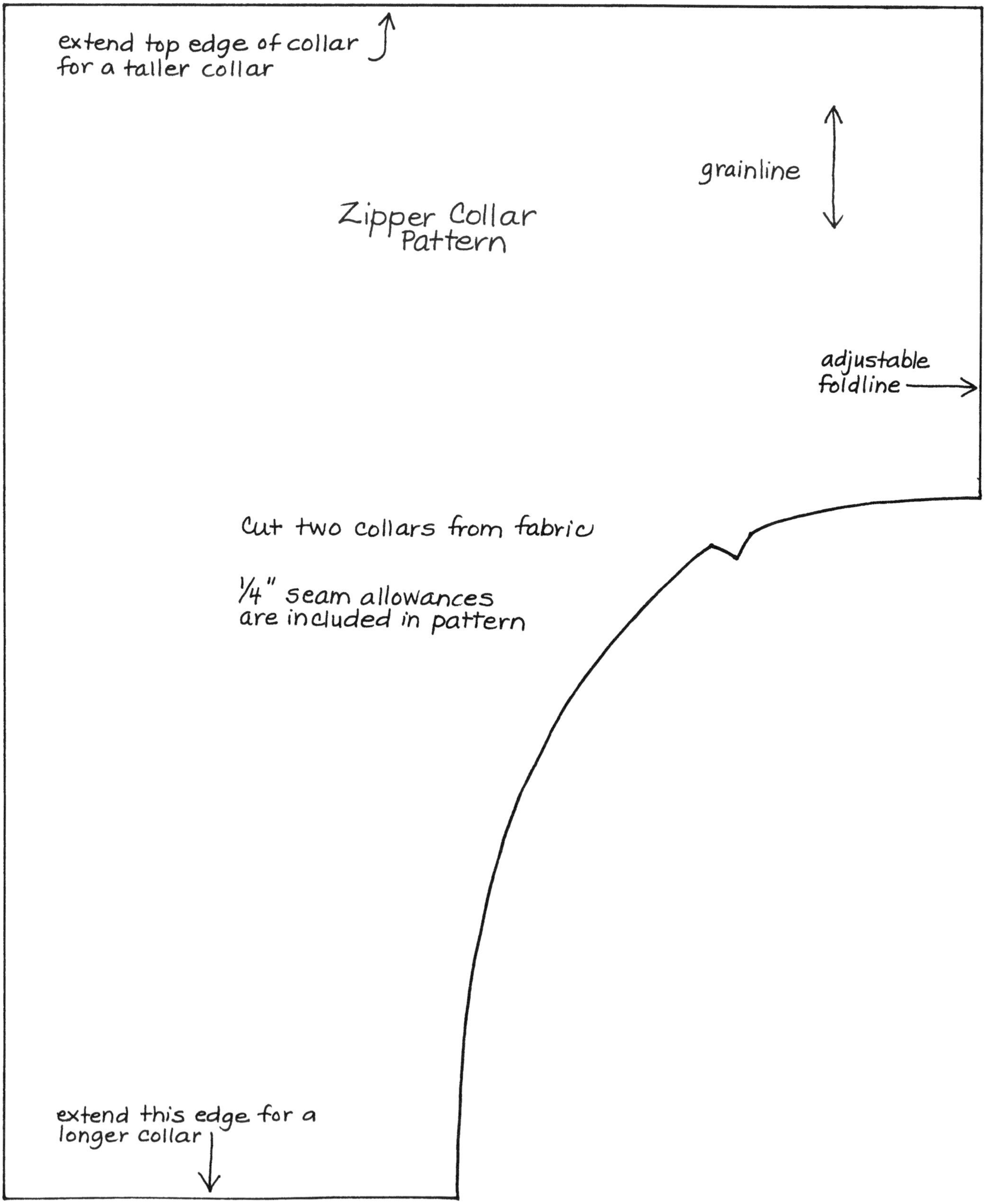

extend top edge of collar
for a taller collar ⤴

grainline ↕

Zipper Collar
Pattern

adjustable
foldline ⟶

Cut two collars from fabric

¼" seam allowances
are included in pattern

extend this edge for a
longer collar ↓

✦ CROSS-OVER RIBBING COLLAR ✦

Since this collar involves removing the bottom ribbing, finish the bottom edge of your shirt using one of the ideas in chapter 4 or on page 44. To create a contrasting effect, use the ribbing from another sweatshirt you have altered.

I created two versions of the cross-over ribbing collar to share with you. The gray sweatshirt shows the Cross-Over Ribbing Collar. To create this collar, I removed the bottom ribbing and cut it to fit the neckline after removing the original neck ribbing. The royal blue sweatshirt has a Two–Polo Collar Neckline (instructions begin on page 20). To form the cross-over collar, I used two polo collars with a seam in the center back of the neckline. Both types of ribbing work well and look great.

Supplies Needed

- one sweatshirt
- 6″ (15cm) ribbing or bottom ribbing cut from sweatshirt

1 For this alteration, enlarge the neck opening by staystitching ½″ (1.3cm) below the neck ribbing and cutting away the original ribbing and the sweatshirt fabric above the stitching line (Fig. 1). See page 61 for more on staystitching.

FIGURE 1. Staystitch ½″ below the neck ribbing all the way around the neck and then cut off the ribbing and extra fabric above the staystitching.

2 Test the size of the neck opening by pulling the sweatshirt on over your head. The opening should be large enough for your head to slip easily through. Measure the size of the new neck opening with the tape measure on edge, as described on page 6.

3 Remove the shirt's bottom ribbing using the instructions on pages 7–8, or work with a separate piece of ribbing. Cut the bottom ribbing open so it is a long strip rather than a circle. Cut a piece of ribbing the length of the entire neck opening. Press to straighten the "ruffles" on the cut edges of the ribbing (Fig. 2). Keep the ribbing folded, with the wrong sides of the fabric together.

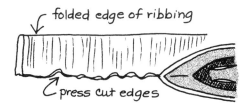

FIGURE 2. Press the raw edges of the folded ribbing.

4 Divide the total neckline measurement into thirds (see the hint on folding the tape measure on page 6) and mark the ⅓ divisions (Fig. 3).

FIGURE 3. Divide the ribbing length in thirds and mark the divisions on the cut edges.

5 Trace the Cross-Over Collar Curve Pattern from the book (Fig. 4) onto paper, and cut it out. Using a chalk marker or washable marking pen, trace the pattern on each end third of the ribbing piece (Fig. 5). Cut the ribbing to the new curved collar shape. Overlap the curved portions to the marks at the ⅓ divisions, and pin the collar together (Fig. 6). Carefully test to see if the ribbing will stretch to fit over your head. If it's a tight fit, unpin the collar and adjust the overlap so the collar band is larger.

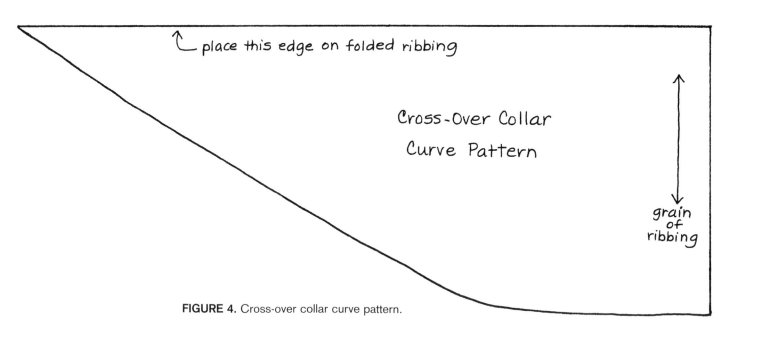

FIGURE 4. Cross-over collar curve pattern.

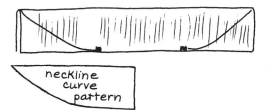

FIGURE 5. Trace the neckline curve pattern on each end of the ribbing.

6 With a chalk marker or a washable marking pen, mark quarter portions on the sweatshirt neckline and on the new collar, using the directions on page 8. Center the overlapped ribbing area on the center front of the shirt (Fig. 7). Pin the collar to the neckline. If the ribbing is difficult to stretch between the pins, unpin the collar and adjust the overlap so the collar band is larger. Sew or serge the collar to the shirt (see page 5). Try on the shirt again to test the neck opening before understitching the seam allowances to the sweatshirt with the method described on page 10.

If you opted to remove the sweatshirt bottom ribbing you'll need to finish the hemline. Refer to chapter 4, "Creative Cuffs, Sleeves, Pockets, and Hems," and select the hemline that works best for you.

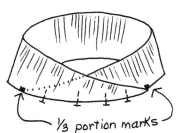

FIGURE 6. Overlap the collar ends, placing the ends at the ⅓ portion marks on the ribbing.

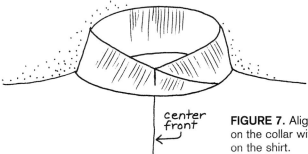

FIGURE 7. Align the overlapped area on the collar with the center front line on the shirt.

✦ TWO-POLO COLLAR ✦ OVERLAPPING NECKLINE

Make an overlapping collar using two polo collars. The collars can be the same color or two different colors, just for fun. Since most polo collars don't stretch quite as much as ribbing fabric, be sure to test the neckline and the final collar shape before sewing it to the sweatshirt.

Supplies Needed

- one sweatshirt
- two polo/finished-edge knit collars

1 Prepare the overlapping collar by sewing the two polo collars together along the short sides (Fig. 1). Use a ⅛" (3mm) seam allowance.

2 Mark the neckline measurement on the collars, centering the measurement on the seamline connecting the two collars (Fig. 2).

3 Proceed with Step 3 of the directions for "Cross-Over Ribbing Collar" to cut and attach the two-piece overlapping collar.

The inspiration for this collar came from a knit shirt I have worn and enjoyed. I liked the lines of the overlapping portions of the collar, so when I realized this feature could be adapted for a sweatshirt, I thought it would be a great addition to this section of the book.

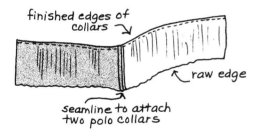

FIGURE 1. Sew two polo collars together with a narrow ⅛" seam allowance.

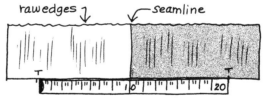
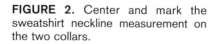

FIGURE 2. Center and mark the sweatshirt neckline measurement on the two collars.

✦ Funnel Collar with Zipper ✦

Adding a zipper to the funnel collar allows you to open or close the neckline for comfort. It's always easiest to work with a zipper that's longer than the actual collar length, cutting off the zipper excess as needed.

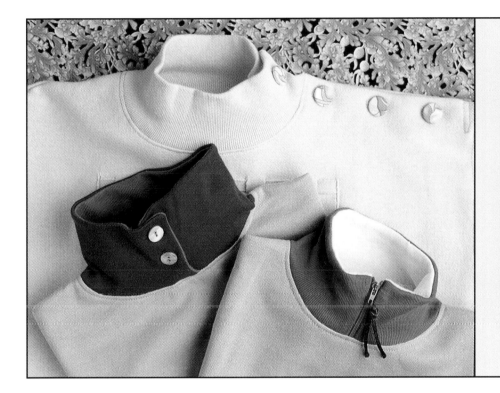

Replace the ordinary crewneck on your sweatshirts with wider, funnel collars—and experiment with different types of closures. If you want to add buttons and buttonholes from the collar to the shoulder seam, see page 24. If you'd rather align the buttons on the sweatshirt's center front, see page 23. In this project, you'll learn to add a zipper to the center front. Because the funnel collar is such an easy alteration to make, I encourage you to try all three versions.

Supplies Needed

- one sweatshirt
- two 3″ (7.5cm) wide (or whatever width you prefer) bands of ribbing
- ¼ yd. (23cm) tear-away stabilizer
- one zipper 4″ (10cm) long or longer
- 4″ (10cm) cord, ribbon, or Ultrasuede (optional)

1 Pull the sweatshirt on over your head to test the neck size. If it is tight, make a larger opening in the neckline: Staystitch ½″ (1.3cm) below the bottom edge of the neck ribbing instead of right next to the edge, using the instructions on page 6. Then, remove the ribbing, cutting away the extra fabric above the staystitching line. Try on the shirt again to test the size of the opening.

2 Measure the neck opening using the instructions on page 6. Calculate ⅔ of the measurement and add 1″ (2.5cm). For example, if your sweatshirt has a neck opening of 21″ (53.5cm), cut the funnel collar ribbing to a length of 15″ (38cm)—⅔ of 21″ (53.5cm) is 14″ (35.5cm) plus 1″ (2.5cm) = 15″ (38cm). For the shirt in the illustration, I used a 3″ (7.5cm) wide band of ribbing, which I cut from the shirt's bottom edge. Remember that the actual height of the collar will be ½″(1.3cm) less than the 3″ (7.5cm) width, because of the two ¼″ (6mm) seam allowances (Fig. 1). Hold the two short ends of the strips together and check the fit over your head.

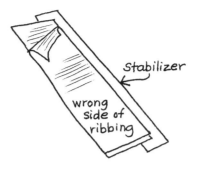

FIGURE 2. Place a piece of stabilizer under the two pieces of ribbing fabric before stitching.

4 Follow the instructions on pages 11–12 to attach the zipper to the two ribbing fabrics.

5 When the zipper collar is ready to be sewn to the shirt, you can place the zipper at center front or to the side, lining it up with a raglan seam if the shirt has one (Fig. 3). Using a chalk marker or a washable marking pen, mark the quarter portions on both the zipper collar and the shirt neckline, as described on page 8. Pin the collar to the neckline, try the shirt on to check the fit, then sew or serge the collar to the sweatshirt. Using the instructions on pages 10–11, follow with a row of understitching to sew the seam allowances to the shirt and complete this new collar treatment.

6 The final touch to this sweatshirt: Add a zipper pull to the hole in the zipper head using a short piece of cord, ribbon, or Ultrasuede.

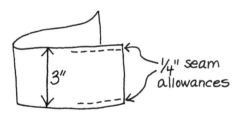

FIGURE 1. Actual collar width less the seam allowances is 2¹/₂″.

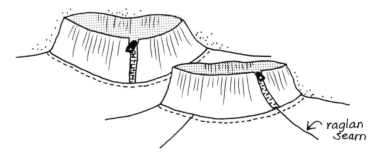

FIGURE 3. Place the collar's zipper opening at the shirt center front or lined up with the raglan seam.

3 Place the two ribbing pieces right sides together with a strip of stabilizer beneath (Fig. 2). Sew the two fabrics together along the top lengthwise edge, using a ½″ (6mm) seam allowance. Remove the stabilizer and press the seam flat and then press it open.

Funnel Collar with Buttons

On this version of the funnel collar, buttons and buttonholes close and trim the ribbing collar. Wear the collar open or buttoned (Fig. 1).

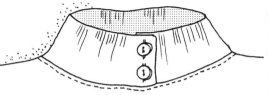

FIGURE 1. Buttons and buttonholes are added to this version of the funnel collar.

Supplies Needed

- one sweatshirt
- ¼ yd. (23cm) knit fabric for collar (interlock or ribbing taken from the bottom of the sweatshirt)
- ¼ yd. (23cm) lightweight fusible interfacing (optional)
- ¼ yd. (23cm) tear-away stabilizer
- small piece of water-soluble stabilizer (optional)
- two buttons

1 Pull the sweatshirt on over your head to test the neck size. If it is tight, make a larger opening in the neckline: Staystitch ½" (1.3cm) below the neck ribbing around the neckline, using the instructions on pages 6–7. Then, remove the ribbing, cutting away the extra fabric above the staystitching line. Try on the shirt again to test the size of the neck opening.

2 Measure the neck opening, using the instructions on page 6. Calculate the length of the knit fabric for the new collar: Use ¾ of the measurement if you are using interlock knit fabric and ⅔ of the measure if you are using ribbing. (Ribbing knits are usually stretchier fabrics, so you won't need as long a piece for the collar as you would for interlock or T-shirt knit.) Add 2" (5cm) to the measurement for the button/buttonhole overlap. Cut two strips of knit 4" (10cm) wide—or another width of your choice—and the length you calculated with an extra 2" (5cm) for the overlap.

3 To stabilize the collar knits, you may want to add lightweight knit interfacing to the collar fabric chosen for the lining or back of the collar. Cut the interfacing with the stretch matching the stretch of the fabric, then position and fuse it ½" (1.3cm) above the bottom edge of the fabric (Fig. 2).

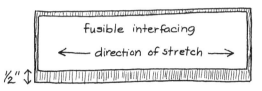

½" ↕

FIGURE 2. On the wrong side of the collar lining, fuse lightweight fusible interfacing, leaving a ½" seam allowance at the bottom edge.

4 Place the two fabrics right sides together with a piece of the tear-away stabilizer slightly larger than the fabric you're stitching on beneath. Sew the sides and across the top edges, using a ¼" (6mm) seam allowance. Remove the stabilizer. Clip the corners, turn the collar right side out, and press (Fig. 3).

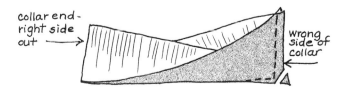

collar end—right side out →

wrong side of collar

FIGURE 3. Sew the collar and lining together with right sides together. Clip the corners, turn the fabrics right side out and press.

5 It's easier to sew the buttonholes now, before you sew the collar to the shirt. Practice the buttonholes on small pieces of the knit fabric first, adding a layer of interfacing if your collar has interfacing. I like to use water-soluble stabilizer under the knit fabrics when I sew buttonholes because it's easiest to remove all traces of the stabilizer (Fig. 4). Keep the buttonhole ends clear of the bottom raw edge of the collar, at least ¾" (2cm) above the raw edges. Cut the buttonholes open.

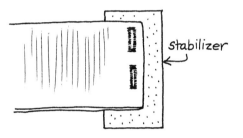

FIGURE 4. Sew the buttonholes on the collar with a piece of stabilizer beneath.

6 Overlap the two ends of the collar 1" (2.5cm) and baste across the bottom edge (Fig. 5). Sew the buttons to the collar.

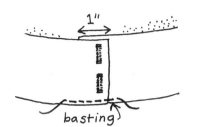

FIGURE 5. Overlap the buttonhole end of the collar over the opposite end by 1" and baste across the bottom edges.

7 Using a chalk marker or a washable marking pen, mark the quarter portions on both the button collar and the shirt neckline, as described on page 8. Match up the quarter marks and pin the collar to the neckline. Sew or serge the two together. Understitch the seam allowances to the shirt using the instructions on pages 10–11.

FUNNEL COLLAR WITH BUTTONS AND SHOULDER OPENING

For this variation on the funnel collar, you'll need to use a sweatshirt with set-in sleeves. A row of buttons begins on the funnel collar and continues onto the shoulder of the sweatshirt. By opening up the neckline and shoulder seam, you'll also gain a very large neck opening to pull over your head. This can make putting on a sweatshirt easier for someone who doesn't like to destroy her hairstyle (Fig. 1).

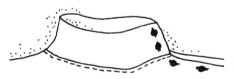

FIGURE 1. This version of the funnel collar features a button/buttonhole closure extending from the collar to the sleeve seam.

 **Supplies Needed**

- one sweatshirt with set-in sleeves
- ¼ yd. (23cm) fabric for shoulder placket
- ⅛ yd. (11.5cm) lightweight fusible interfacing
- small piece of water-soluble stabilizer (optional)
- four to six buttons

1 Staystitch around the sweatshirt neckline and cut away the original ribbing and extra fabric above the stitching line, using the instructions on pages 6–7.

2 On the shoulder edge where you plan to add the placket (I usually use the right side, as you are looking at the shirt front), carefully open the stitching all the way to the sleeve seam (Fig. 2). Press the seam allowance edges flat, and measure the opening for the placket from the edge of the neckline to the sleeve seam. Double the measurement of the opening and add 1" (2.5cm) to determine the length of the placket fabric. For example, my shoulder opening measured 7" (18cm), so I cut the placket fabric 15" (38cm) long (Fig. 3).

3 Cut a strip of fabric using the number you calculated in Step 2 for the placket length and 3" (7.5cm) for the width. If the fabric is soft and you want to give it more stability, fuse lightweight interfacing to the wrong side of the fabric. Fold and press the fabric in half, with wrong sides together, meeting the long raw edges (Fig. 4).

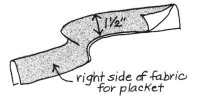

FIGURE 4. Fold and press the 3" wide placket fabric in half, meeting wrong sides.

4 Pin the cut edges of the placket to the shoulder seam allowances, starting on one side of the opening and continuing to the other side. Sew the placket in place by stitching on the sweatshirt side, using the same seam allowance used for the shoulder seam. On most shirts, this will be a very narrow seam allowance. At the center, swivel the fabrics around so you can continue sewing directly to the other side of the shoulder opening (Fig. 5).

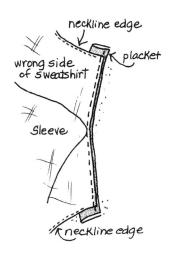

FIGURE 5. Sew the placket strip to the shoulder opening by sewing on the wrong side of the sweatshirt to use the same seam allowances used for the shoulder seam you cut open.

5 Press the seam and understitch the seam allowances to the placket fabric, using the instructions on pages 10–11. Turn the placket on the front side of the shirt inside to form the hidden placket (Fig. 6).

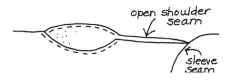

FIGURE 2. After staystitching around the neckline, open the shoulder seam.

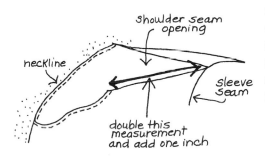

FIGURE 3. Measure the length of the shoulder opening, double the measurement, and add 1".

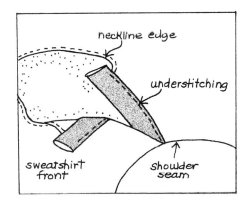

FIGURE 6. Understitch the seam allowances to the placket fabric and turn the placket on the front shoulder inside the opening.

6 Sew a rectangle through the sweatshirt and the placket fabrics at the sleeve end of the placket (Fig. 7).

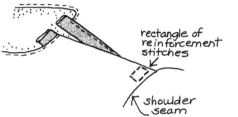

FIGURE 7. Sew through the sweatshirt and all layers of the placket to secure the end of the placket.

7 The next step is making the funnel collar. Remove the bottom sweatshirt ribbing as explained on page 7. Cut the circle of ribbing open so it is a long strip. Press the raw edges to flatten them.

8 Measure the open neckline of the sweatshirt using the instructions on page 6, and cut a piece of the bottom ribbing to a length ⅔ of the neck measurement plus ½" (1.3cm) for seam allowances. Fuse a small piece of tricot knit interfacing near both ends of the ribbing on the wrong side of the fabric (Fig. 8). The interfacing will support the buttons and buttonholes that you will attach later.

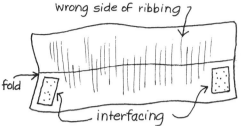

FIGURE 8. Fuse small pieces of tricot knit interfacing to the ends of the ribbing strip on the wrong side of the ribbing. The interfacing will give extra strength to the ribbing for the buttonholes and buttons to be added.

9 With right sides of the folded ribbing together and a piece of stabilizer underneath, sew the short ends together with a ¼" (6mm) seam allowance (Fig. 9). Turn the collar right side out and press the bottom edges. You may need to trim away the seam allowances if the edges and corners of the collar are too bulky or thick. To test the collar size, wrap it around your neck with a 1" (2.5cm) overlap.

FIGURE 9. Fold the ribbing with right sides together and sew across the ends.

10 With a chalk marker or washable marking pen, mark the quarter portions on both the collar and the shirt neckline, using the instructions

on page 8. The two collar edges will be lined up with the placket ends on the sweatshirt shoulder line (Fig. 10). Pin the collar to the sweatshirt neckline and sew it to the sweatshirt, the right sides of the fabric together, using a ¼" (6mm) seam allowance. Take time and care in matching up and sewing the collar ends to the sweatshirt, so you will have a very neat-looking collar attachment. Follow by understitching the seam allowances to the shirt, as described on pages 10–11.

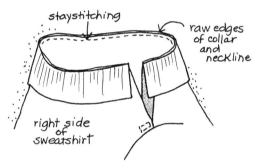

FIGURE 10. Place the raw edges of the collar on the sweatshirt neckline, with the collar ends meeting the placket ends.

11 Plan and space the buttonholes on the collar and placket, remembering to keep the last buttonhole ½" (1.3cm) from the finished edge. Sew the buttonholes and buttons to the sweatshirt. Practice the buttonholes on scraps of fabric before you work on the sweatshirt. Add a piece of stabilizer under the neck ribbing and placket opening before sewing the buttonholes (Fig. 11). Cut the buttonholes open and sew the buttons to the collar and inside the placket.

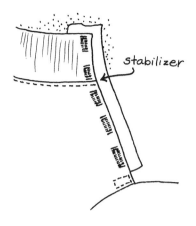

FIGURE 11. Be sure to place a piece of stabilizer under the buttonhole side of the placket before sewing the buttonholes. Remove the stabilizer when you've finished sewing.

Now that you've completed the neckline, it's time to finish the hem. There are a number of different styles to choose from. Simply turn to chapter 4, "Creative Cuffs, Sleeves, Pockets, and Hems," and select the style that works best for you.

FUNNEL DRAWSTRING COLLAR

This neckline was invented to solve a problem. A sweatshirt I purchased and didn't try on first had an incredibly small neck opening. To fix it, I staystitched 1″ (2.5cm) around the neck ribbing, cut away the original ribbing, and added a funnel drawstring collar (Fig. 1).

Here are two funnel collars that feature various fabrics. On the left, the thermal knit collar is topped with a green knit casing for a drawstring closure. I removed the black sweatshirt's original neckline and replaced it with a flannel funnel collar cut on the bias and ringed with a piece of black Lycra fabric to form a drawstring (see instructions on page 29.) I used felt from Kunin Felt for the cabin/trees design and included the applique designs from the shirts on pages 83 and 146 in case you'd like to add them to your newly altered sweatshirt.

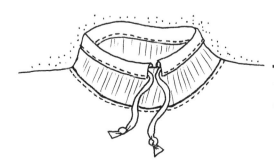

FIGURE 1. This funnel collar is topped with a casing and a drawstring.

Supplies Needed

- one sweatshirt
- ¼ yd.(23cm) knit fabric for the funnel collar (e.g., ribbing, interlock knit, sweatshirt fleece)
- 2″ (5cm) strip of contrasting color knit fabric for casing
- ⅔ yd. (61cm) cord or ribbon for drawstring

1 Check the neck opening before beginning this alteration. You, too, may want to enlarge the neck by staystitching farther from the neck ribbing, for example, another ½″ (1.3cm) down. Then, cut away the ribbing and extra fabric above the staystitching line, using the directions on page 6.

2 Measure the new neck opening, using the instructions on page 6. Select a knit fabric for the collar: Possibilities include ribbing, interlock knit, and sweatshirt fleece. For ribbing, calculate ⅔ of the neck measure, for interlock knit and fleece ¾ of the measure. Add ½″ (1.3cm) to your measurement for seam allowances. The width of the collar fabric is 6½″ (17cm), with a fold in the center so the collar is actually 3″ (7.5cm) wide upon completion, with ¼″ (6mm) seam allowances. Of course, you can change this measurement to a collar size of your choice. After cutting the fabric for the collar, stretch the fabric around your head to test the fit (Fig. 2).

FIGURE 2. Test the length of the knit fabric by stretching it around your head. It should easily stretch so the ends meet.

3 With the right sides of the fabric facing each other, sew the short ends together, with a ¼″ (6mm) seam allowance. Press the seam and fold the fabric in half so the right side is facing out. Pin the raw edges together at the bottom of the collar (Fig. 3).

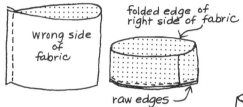

FIGURE 3. Sew the collar fabric into a tube, fold it in half with wrong sides together, and baste the raw edges together.

4 Add the casing to the upper collar edge at this time, or wait until the collar is sewn to the shirt. Measure around the folded edge of the collar using the instructions on page 6, and cut a 2″ (5cm) wide strip of contrasting color knit fabric to that measurement. Turn under and fuse or sew ¼″ (6mm) seam allowances on the short ends of the fabric strip (Fig. 4).

FIGURE 4. Cut a casing for the folded edge of the collar and turn under the ends ¼″ and sew in place.

5 With the right side of the strip facing the right side of the collar, begin pinning the strip to the collar ¼″ (6mm) away from the center front line of the upper collar edge. There will be a small gap at center front when the entire strip is pinned in place (Fig. 5). Sew with a ¼″ (6mm) seam allowance to attach the casing strip.

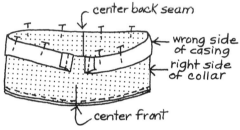

FIGURE 5. Pin the casing strip to the upper edge of the collar.

6 Fold the raw edge of the strip over the collar to the back side to create the casing. Pin the edge in place with pins and "stitch in the ditch" on the right side of the collar to secure the casing (Fig. 6). After stitching, you may want to trim away some of the excess knit fabric on the back side of the casing.

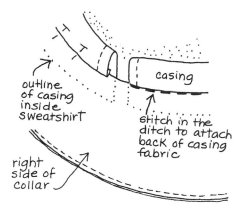

outline
of casing
inside
sweatshirt

casing

stitch in the
ditch to attach
back of casing
fabric

right
side of
collar

FIGURE 6. Make a casing by turning the loose edge of the fabric to the wrong side of the collar. Pin and stitch in the ditch to hold the casing in place.

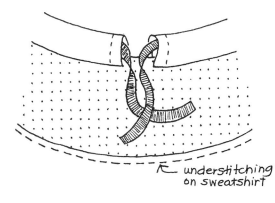

understitching
on sweatshirt

FIGURE 7. Sew the collar to the sweatshirt neckline and understitch the seam allowances to the shirt. Add a drawstring inside the casing.

7 With the chalk marker or a washable marking pen, mark the quarter portions of both the collar and the sweatshirt neckline as explained on page 8. Place the seam of the collar at the center back of the shirt. Pin the collar to the neckline, and sew or serge the collar to the sweatshirt with a ¼" (6mm) seam allowance. Add a row of understitching to secure the seam allowances to the shirt, using the instructions on page 10.

8 Insert a piece of cord or ribbon into the collar casing and your new sweatshirt funnel collar is complete (Fig. 7).

FUNNEL COLLAR WITH WOVEN (NON-STRETCH) FABRIC

Cut on the bias, the funnel collar can be adapted for non-stretch fabrics to take advantage of a variety of prints and colors. I used plaid flannel for the illustration and cut the fabric on the bias to give some "stretch" to the woven fabric (Fig. 1).

FIGURE 1. Funnel collar in woven fabric cut on the bias.

 ## Supplies Needed

- one sweatshirt
- 1 yd. (91.5cm) woven fabric
- 2" (5cm) strip of Lycra or other non-fray fabric for casing
- 1 yd. (91.5cm) cord or ribbon for drawstring

1 To add a funnel collar of non-stretch fabric, it is necessary to enlarge the neckline of the sweatshirt. Staystitch around the neckline, using the instructions on page 6. For example, I staystitched ½″ (1.3cm) from the back neck ribbing and dipped to 1″ (2.5cm) below the front neck ribbing (Fig. 2). You can enlarge the neckline to your own preferences.

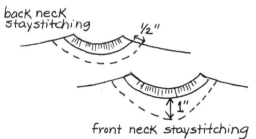

FIGURE 2. Staystitch around the back neckline ½″ from the ribbing edge. On the front, staystitch to 1″ below the neck ribbing at center front.

2 Cut away the original ribbing and the extra sweatshirt fabric above the stitching line. Pull on the shirt over your head. It should pull over easily. If it doesn't, staystitch again, a bit farther from your first row, for example another ½″ (1.3cm) down. Then, trim away the excess fabric close to the second stitching (Fig. 3).

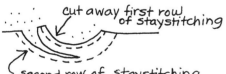

FIGURE 3. To make the neck opening larger, add a second row of staystitching and then cut away the first row of staystitching.

3 Measure the neck opening for the funnel fabric, using the instructions on page 6.

▶ If using the fabric across the grain, cut the collar the same length as the neck opening plus an extra ½″ (1.3cm) for seam allowances.

▶ If using fabric cut on the bias, fold the corner of the fabric over to form a triangle in the fabric (Fig. 4). From the fold I measured 5″ (12.5cm) for the height of the collar and then the length of the collar is 1″ (2.5cm) less than the actual neckline measurement. There is some stretch to the bias, so it will fit easily into the neckline. Cut the fabric piece from the fabric and wrap it around your head to see if it's large enough.

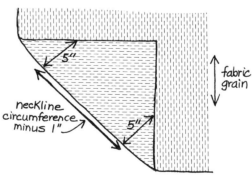

FIGURE 4. Fold the fabric diagonally across the grain, allowing for the measurements of the collar. This placement will yield a bias cut collar for a sweatshirt.

4 To form the collar, meet the side edges with right sides of the fabric together. Sew the fabric into a tube, using a ¼″ (6mm) seam allowance. Press the seam. Turn the fabric right side out and fold it in half, bringing the raw edges together.

You can leave the collar as is, or you can add the casing and drawstring to the top folded edge, using the instructions given in Steps 4 through 6 for the Funnel Drawstring Collar (page 28).

5 Using a chalk marker or a washable marking pen, mark the quarter portions on both the new collar and the shirt neckline, as described on page 8. Place the collar seam at center back of the neckline. Pin the collar to the neckline, and sew the it to the shirt with a ¼″ (6mm) seam allowance. Understitch the seam allowances to the sweatshirt, following the instructions on page 10.

As you can tell, the funnel collar is versatile and adaptable in its size and style of closure. Removing the original sweatshirt crew ribbing neckline and adding a funnel collar will change the ordinary look of the sweatshirt and add a touch of style. It may be the only thing you'll want to do to improve the sweatshirt!

✦ TWO-PIECE POLO ✦ COLLAR NECKLINE

This neckline is a little different and offers an interesting change from a traditional crew ribbing neckline. Polo collars are usually not as stretchy as ribbing, so I've enlarged the sweatshirt neckline a bit to accommodate this new collar.

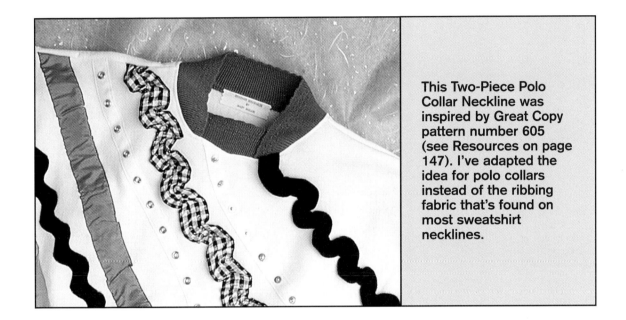

This Two-Piece Polo Collar Neckline was inspired by Great Copy pattern number 605 (see Resources on page 147). I've adapted the idea for polo collars instead of the ribbing fabric that's found on most sweatshirt necklines.

Supplies Needed

- one sweatshirt
- two polo/finished-edge knit collars

1 Staystitch ½" (1.3cm) below the neck ribbing of the sweatshirt, following the directions on page 6. Cut off the ribbing and the sweatshirt fabric right above the stitching line. Try the shirt on to make sure that the neck opening is large enough to slip easily over your head. If it isn't, sew an-

other row of staystitching ¼" (6mm) away from the first stitching line and cut away the fabric above the new stitching.

2 Measure around the neckline and calculate ⅔ of the measurement, using the instructions on page 6. This will be the length of the main, or larger, collar piece. Select one of your two collars to be the main piece, and measure and mark this length on the finished collar edge, using a chalk marker or washable marking pen (Fig. 1).

Main Polo Collar:

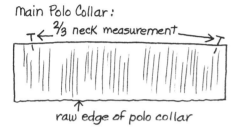

FIGURE 1. Measure and mark ⅔ of the sweatshirt neck measurement on the main polo collar.

3 Trace the Small Front Collar Pattern from the book (Fig. 2) onto a piece of paper, and cut it out. Place the straight edge of the pattern along the finished edge of one collar, trace it, cut it out, and mark the two notches on the collar (Fig. 3).

Polo Collar for Small Front Section:

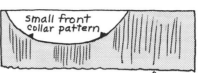

raw edge of collar ↑

FIGURE 3. Place the small front collar pattern on the finished edge of the second polo collar, cut it out, and mark the notches.

4 On the main polo collar, use the curved edge of the pattern to draw the shape at each end of the measured length. Trace the collar pattern ends, marking the notches, and connect the line between (Fig. 4). Cut out the main collar piece.

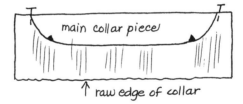

↑ raw edge of collar

FIGURE 4. Trace the curved edges of the small collar pattern on the main collar and mark the notches.

5 Overlap the two collar parts, matching the notches (Fig. 5). Pin the collar ends together. Try the shirt on to test the fit. If the opening is too small, readjust the overlap.

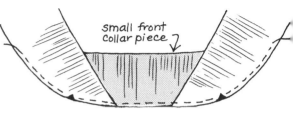

FIGURE 5. Match the notches of the two collar sections and baste together.

6 Using a chalk marker or a washable marking pen, mark the quarter portions on both the new collar and the shirt neckline, as described on page 8. Pin the collar to the neckline, and sew or serge the collar to the shirt, using a ¼″ (6mm) seam allowance.

7 Press and understitch the seam allowances to the shirt, using the directions on pages 10–11.

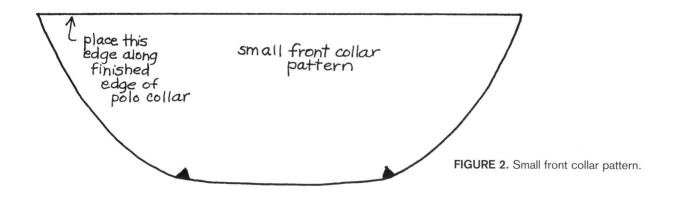

FIGURE 2. Small front collar pattern.

✦ U Neck with Insert ✦

For this good-looking treatment, the ribbing in the neckline is created either from the ribbing at the bottom edge of the sweatshirt or from new ribbing fabric. Once you've chosen the ribbing, select a coordinating fabric for the insert.

It's not exactly a V neck, but it's close, so I named it a U neck. I added a wide band of ribbing to encircle the neckline and a woven fabric insert to provide the finishing touch. The enlarged opening in the sweatshirt provides a more comfortable neckline with a touch of style. The insert fabric is by VIP.

Supplies Needed

- one sweatshirt
- sweatshirt bottom ribbing or ¼ yd. (23cm) ribbing fabric
- 8″ × 12″ (20.5 × 30.5cm) piece of coordinating knit or woven fabric

1 Using a chalk marker or washable marking pen, draw a line on the sweatshirt center front to 7″ (18cm) below the bottom of the neck ribbing. Across the center front line, draw a perpendicular line as long as the measure of two widths of the ribbing to be used. For example, the ribbing piece I used from the bottom edge of another sweatshirt was 3″

(7.5cm) wide, so I centered the 6″ (15cm) line on the center front line (Fig. 1).

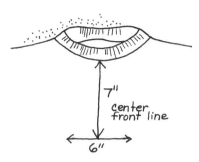

FIGURE 1. On the shirt's center front, measure down 7″. Draw a horizontal line of 6″, centered on the 7″ line.

2 From the shoulder edge of each side of the neck ribbing, at least ¼″ (6mm) from the ribbing, draw a line to the end of the horizontal line near the shirt's center (Fig. 2). This will form the U "frame" of the ribbing insertion.

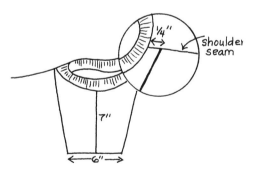

FIGURE 2. Draw a line from the edge of the neck ribbing to the end of the 6″ line to form the frame for the ribbing neckline.

3 Staystitch on the lines and around the back of the sweatshirt neck, using the instructions on pages 6–7. Cut away the ribbing and the fleece fabric inside the staystitching line, leaving ¼″ (6mm) on the sides and the back of the neck and ½″(1.3cm) above the horizontal staystitching line (Fig. 3).

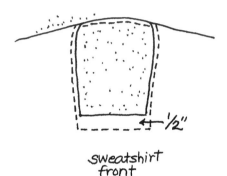

FIGURE 3. Staystitch on the lines drawn on the shirt front and also around the shirt back neckline. Cut away the fabric inside the stitching line, leaving ½″ across the bottom edge of the neck opening.

4 Measure the new neck opening along the staystitching line, using the technique on page 6. Start at the bottom of one side, then continue around the neck and down the other side (Fig. 4). Cut a band of ribbing to ¾″ of the measurement. To do this calculation quickly, fold the tape measure in fourths, as described on page 6.

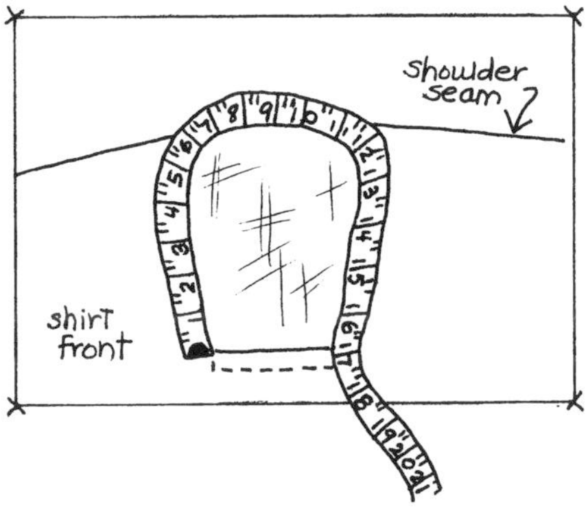

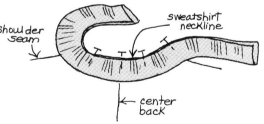

FIGURE 4. Measure the sides and back of the neck opening with a tape measure.

5 Pin the center of the ribbing band (raw edges meeting shirt neck raw edge) to the center of the back. Stretch the ribbing slightly and pin to each shoulder or raglan seam (Fig. 5). This stretching across the back neckline will ensure that the ribbing will lie flat against the body, rather than stand away from it. Pin several more times between the center back and the shoulder pins.

FIGURE 5. Begin pinning the ribbing to the sweatshirt neckline at center back.

6 Continue to pin the ribbing down each side of the opening, making sure the ends overlap the staystitching line across the bottom of the opening (Fig. 6). Sew the ribbing to the shirt with ¼" (6mm) seam allowances. Press the seam.

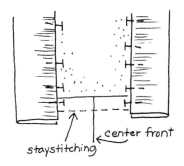

FIGURE 6. Pin the ribbing down each side of the front opening, making sure the ends extend past the horizontal front staystitching.

7 Working on the wrong side of the shirt, make diagonal cuts to the inside corners of the staystitching lines (Fig. 7).

FIGURE 7. Cut diagonally to the corners of the staystitching of the neckline frame.

Turn the ribbing inside the neck opening. Pin the two ribbing ends to the ½" (1.3cm) seam allowance on the shirt

and sew across, making sure the ends of the stitching lines meet on the sides of the opening (Fig. 8).

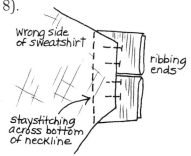

FIGURE 8. Sew across the sweatshirt neckline staystitching to attach the ribbing ends to the sweatshirt.

8 Try on the shirt to determine the size and placement of the fabric insert. Slide a piece of paper beneath the ribbing to substitute for the fabric and pin it into place to mark the location for the insert (Fig. 9). Remove the shirt and measure the paper and sweatshirt so you can cut an insert to fit. Keep in mind that the insert should be wider and longer than the insert area.

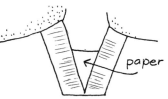

FIGURE 9. Try on the shirt and slide a piece of paper inside the neckline to determine the location and size of the fabric insert.

9 Fold the insert fabric at the top edge (Fig. 10). Place it inside the opening and pin it with plenty of pins from the right side of the shirt.

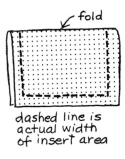

FIGURE 10. Cut the insert fabric on folded fabric, adding extra fabric for the width and length of the actual insert measurement.

Understitch around the entire neckline to secure the seam allowances and insert in place, using the instructions on page 10 (Fig. 11). Try on the shirt and check the insert. Despite careful measuring and sewing, you may need to readjust the insert so it lies flat. (I report this based on experience!)

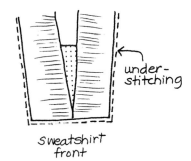

FIGURE 11. Understitch the seam allowance around the entire neckline and at the same time, sew the insert in place.

For someone who likes to wear a more open neckline, the U neck offers comfort with a touch of style.

✦ NECKLINE WITH A DICKEY ✦

Many of my readers and students report that they prefer to wear sweatshirts with collars, so I hope this neckline alteration fits the bill. You can find dickeys in with the accessories and scarves in department stores, or you can make your own.

This change is quick and easy to make with a purchased dickey, and even gives the sweatshirt a nice layered look. In the sweatshirt pictured, I used a dickey that buttons up the front with a polo collar neckline, but consider turtleneck and mock turtleneck dickeys, too.

Supplies Needed

● one sweatshirt
● one knit dickey

1 Try on the sweatshirt and the dickey separately to test the neck sizes of each. If the neck opening of the sweatshirt is too tight to consider adding a dickey, you can convert the neck to a circle neckline and then add the dickey. (See "Circle Neckline with Fabric Insert" on page 40.)

2 With a chalk marker or washable marking pen, mark the center front line on the sweatshirt and the dickey, using the instructions on page 5.

3 Line up the dickey shoulder seams with the sweatshirt shoulder seams. Then, line up the dickey center front line with the sweatshirt center front line. Pin the dickey to the sweatshirt with many pins. This is most accurately and easily done on a dressmaker's dummy or on a real body. (If your friend is serving as a model, you'll save your relationship by

not calling her the "dummy" and also by pinning carefully!) (Fig. 1).

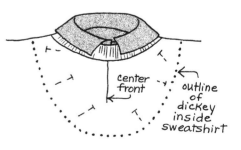

FIGURE 1. Pin the dickey inside the sweatshirt, matching shoulder lines and center front and back on both the dickey and sweatshirt.

4 Remove the sweatshirt from the model. If the dickey has a button front, pin the two overlapping sides and cut away any buttons that might be in line with the "ditch" area where you will sew the dickey to the sweatshirt (Fig. 2).

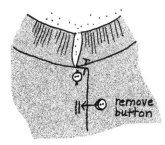

FIGURE 2. Cut off any buttons that might be in the way of the stitching to attach the dickey to the sweatshirt neckline.

5 Add more pins to the "ditch" all the way around the neck (Fig. 3), then prepare to sew the dickey to the shirt. The top thread in the sewing machine should match the color of the sweatshirt. The bobbin thread should match the color of the dickey.

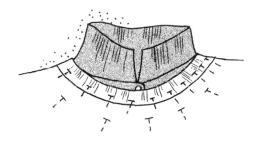

FIGURE 3. Pin the dickey and the shirt together, with many pins around the bottom of the ribbing.

6 You'll appreciate an open arm on your sewing machine when it's time to sew the dickey into the neckline. A "repeater" straight stitch that sews two stitches forward and one stitch back is a good choice for sewing in the neckline, because it allows the seam to stretch as you pull your head through the neckline. If you don't have a straight, repeating stitch, reduce the straight stitch length and pull slightly on the fabrics in front and back of the needle as you sew in the "ditch" (Fig. 4).

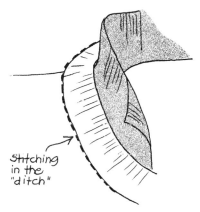

FIGURE 4. Attach the dickey to the sweatshirt by stitching in the ditch.

7 After sewing around the neckline, turn to the inside of the sweatshirt and trim away the excess fabric below the stitching line. On the back of the sweatshirt you can create a neat appearance by leaving 2" (5cm) of extra fabric beyond

the stitching line. Carefully stitch along the curved edge of the dickey's back edge, from shoulder to shoulder, to secure it to the sweatshirt, making sure that the bobbin thread matches the sweatshirt color (Fig. 5). This stitching detail imitates ready-to-wear clothing that has a deeper back facing stitched to the garment.

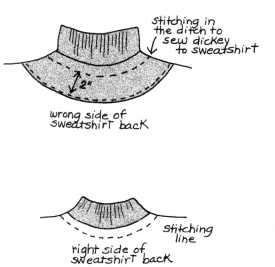

FIGURE 5. Sew another line of stitches 2" below the stitching on the shirt's back neckline, and cut away the dickey beneath the stitching line.

8 Save the extra fabric you cut from the dickey. It may be useful for coordinating appliques for the sweatshirt.

To make your own dickey from a button front shirt, see steps 14–20 on page 134.

✦ CIRCLE NECKLINE ✦ WITH RUNNING STITCHES

If you don't care for the constricting feeling of a regular sweatshirt neckline, you'll be sure to like this alteration—and what's more, it's also easy to do. Don't worry if all your stitches aren't exactly the same size—the effect is charming.

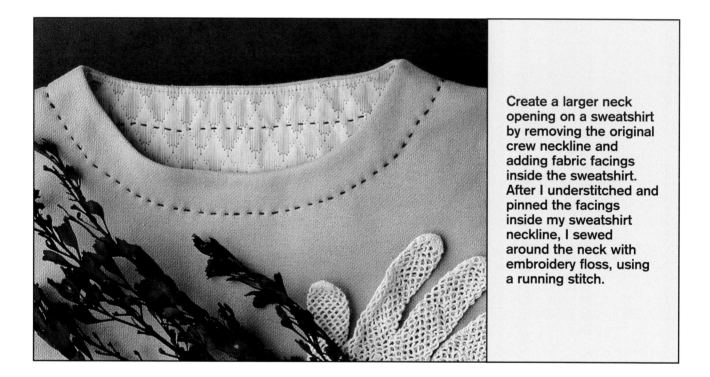

Create a larger neck opening on a sweatshirt by removing the original crew neckline and adding fabric facings inside the sweatshirt. After I understitched and pinned the facings inside my sweatshirt neckline, I sewed around the neck with embroidery floss, using a running stitch.

Supplies Needed

- one sweatshirt
- ¼ yd. (23cm) fabric for facings
- ½ yd. (46cm) lightweight fusible interfacing (optional)
- crochet thread or three strands of embroidery floss for running stitches

1 Staystitch ½″ (1.3cm) below the neck ribbing, using the instructions on page 6. Cut away the ribbing and the extra sweatshirt fabric ¼″ (6mm) above the staystitching line.

2 Fold the sweatshirt neckline in half, meeting the shoulder or raglan seams and pinning them together. Then, follow the instructions for making facings on page 9 to draw and construct the facing to fit the neckline of the sweatshirt.

3 With the right side of the facing to the right side of the sweatshirt, pin the facing to the neckline by matching the shoulder seams, center front, and center back, and sew it on with a ¼″ (6mm) seam allowance (Fig. 1). Press the seam and clip it or trim the seam allowance with a pinking shears to trim and clip it all in one step. Press the seam allowances toward the facing and then understitch the allowances to the facing. Press the facing inside the shirt neckline and secure it by stitching in the shoulder or raglan seams (Fig. 2).

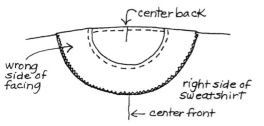

FIGURE 1. Pin and sew the facing to the shirt neckline, meeting the right side of the fabric to the shirt's right side.

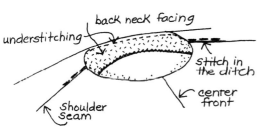

FIGURE 2. Understitch the neckline seam allowance to the facing, press the facing and then stitch in the ditch to hold the facing in place inside the neckline.

4 Now it's time to add the running stitch detail. First mark below the shirt neckline 1″ (2.5cm) all the way around. Using a chalk marker or washable marking pen, draw a con-

tinuous line all the way around, connecting the 1″ (2.5cm) marks. Pin the neckline above and below the marks to secure the facings to the shirt while you sew (Fig. 3).

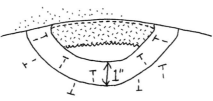

FIGURE 3. Draw a line 1″ from the neck edge and pin the facing and sweatshirt together to prepare for handstitching.

5 Use a sharps or embroidery hand needle and either crochet thread or three strands of embroidery floss for a noticeable running stitch around the neckline. Follow the line drawn on the shirt and hand sew with a running stitch all around the neck, keeping knots on the underside (Fig. 4).

Relax while you stitch and don't worry about each stitch looking exactly alike. After every few stitches, stop and adjust the stitches to make sure you are not pulling the thread too tight. At the end, before knotting, check the sewing again to make sure the stitches are lying flat and are not pulling the sweatshirt and facing fabrics. Press the neckline.

Use this running stitch trim on faced hem and cuff edges too. See the Mitten Gallery on page 111, with its running stitch trim on all the faced edges as well as the center front applique trim.

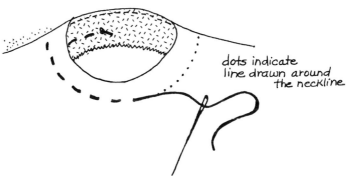

FIGURE 4. Sew a running stitch by hand on the line drawn around the neckline.

CIRCLE NECKLINE WITH FABRIC INSERT

In this sweatshirt, enlarging the neckline becomes an opportunity for adding decoration. Use up coordinating scraps for the facing and inset.

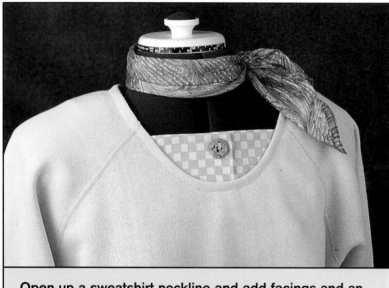

Open up a sweatshirt neckline and add facings and an insert to give your shirt a layered look and a touch of trim. A single button gives the appearance of a button-front opening on the insert.

page 5 (Fig. 1). Trace the Curved Neckline Template from the book (Fig. 2), or draw it freehand, onto a piece of paper and cut it out. Using a chalk marker or a washable marking pen, trace the edges of the template onto the sweatshirt to set the curved edges of the neckline. If you find that you want the curved neckline to be even lower after trying the shirt on, simply place the template lower on the shirt and retrace the edges.

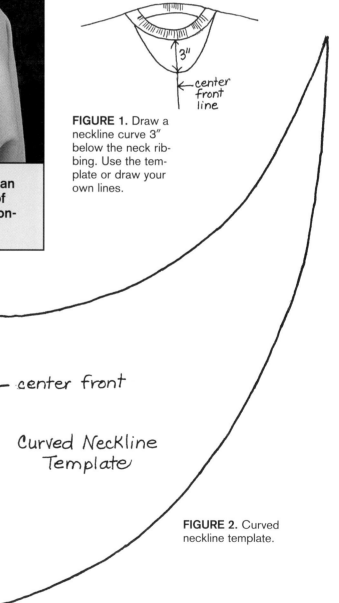

FIGURE 1. Draw a neckline curve 3″ below the neck ribbing. Use the template or draw your own lines.

FIGURE 2. Curved neckline template.

Supplies Needed

- one sweatshirt
- ½ yd. (46cm) fabric for facing and insert
- ½ yd. (46cm) lightweight fusible interfacing (optional)

1 Using a chalk marker or washable marking pen, mark the sweatshirt center front 3″ (7.5cm) down from the neck ribbing, using the technique on

2 Using the instructions on pages 6–7, staystitch along the curved line you drew on the shirt front and continue stitching around the shirt back neckline ¼″ from the bottom of the neck ribbing. Cut away the ribbing and fabric inside the stitching line, leaving a ¼″ (6mm) seam allowance above the staystitching line (Fig. 3). Now try on the shirt to check the scoop neckline. Remember that you will be adding the fabric insert across the opening.

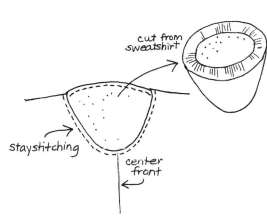

FIGURE 3. Cut off the ribbing and the sweatshirt front fabric ¼″ from the staystitching line.

3 Follow the instructions on page 9 and make facings for the front and back: Use a 4″ (10cm) length at the center front and back and taper to 3″ (7.5cm) at the shoulder areas (Fig. 4). The extra fabric length in the front will allow extra facing fabric in case you decide to sew a deeper scoop in the shirt's front neckline. The back extension imitates ready-to-wear garments, which often fea-

ture a deeper back facing. Cut the facing from the fabric and add lightweight fusible interfacing. Zigzag or serge the outer edge of the facing (Fig. 5).

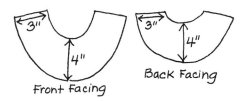

FIGURE 4. Make facing patterns for the sweatshirt neckline.

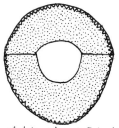

right side of fabric

FIGURE 5. Sew the front and back neck facings together and serge or zigzag around the edges.

4 Match the shoulder seams and the center front and back on the facing and the shirt and pin them together. Sew the right side of the facing to the right side of the shirt neckline with a ¼″ (6mm) seam allowance. For a contrast on the shirt photographed, I chose to use the wrong side of the insert fabric as the right side of the facing.

5 Trim and clip the seam allowance or trim it with pinking shears (my preference

because it accomplishes both jobs at once). Turn the facing to the inside of the shirt, press, and try the shirt on. If you want a deeper neckline, re-sew from the shoulder edges down into the shirt. Then trim and clip the seam allowance again. Press the seams. Understitch the seam allowances to the facings, using the technique on page 10.

6 Try on the shirt again to determine the size and the placement of the fabric insert. Slide a piece of paper into the shirt's neckline and pin it to the sweatshirt. If the sweatshirt has raglan seams, you can line the insert up with the two seams. Mark the desired location of the insert top edges with pins on each side of the shirt neckline before you take it off (Fig. 6).

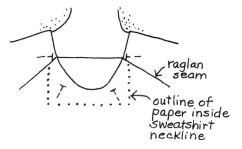

FIGURE 6. With the sweatshirt on, place a piece of paper inside the neckline at the level where you want the top of the insert to be, possibly on a line level with the raglan seams. Pin the paper to the sweatshirt and also place pins to mark the top edge of the insert.

7 With the sweatshirt flat on a table, trace inside the neckline curve on the paper and then remove the paper from the shirt. Add 1″ (2.5cm) around the curved edges of the insert outline to make a pattern for the insert pieces (Fig. 7).

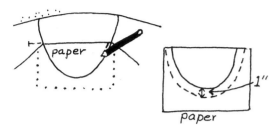

FIGURE 7. Trace the neckline curve on the paper. To make the insert pattern, add 1″ around the curved line.

8 Fold the insert shape in half and place the folded edge 1″ (2.5cm) away from the fold on a piece of fabric (Fig. 8). Cut two insert pieces in this way so they will overlap in the neckline.

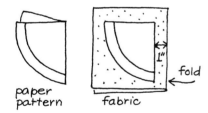

FIGURE 8. Place the paper pattern, folded in half, 1″ from the folded edge of a piece of fabric. Cut the second half of the insert from another piece of folded fabric.

9 With right sides of the insert fabric together, sew across the top straight edges of each insert piece (Fig. 9). Turn the fabrics right side out and press. Overlap the two pieces 1″ (2.5cm) and baste in place (Fig. 10).

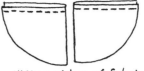

FIGURE 9. Fold the insert fabrics with right sides together and sew across the top straight edges.

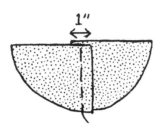

FIGURE 10. The left insert fabric overlaps the right side by 1″. Baste in place.

10 Place the insert inside the neckline and pin in place. Try on the shirt to make sure the insert is correctly placed. Use plenty of pins and continue pinning all the way around the neck to prepare for topstitching (Fig. 11).

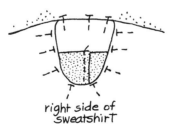

FIGURE 11. Pin the insert inside the sweatshirt and continue to pin all around the neckline to hold the facing in place.

11 Carefully topstitch around the entire neckline, leaving a ½″ (1.3cm) seam

allowance (Fig. 12). This will secure both the insert and the facings. Remove the basting stitches from the insert. Sew in a buttonhole and button, or just a button through both layers of the insert (Fig. 13).

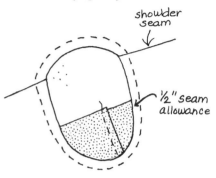

FIGURE 12. Topstitch with a ½″ seam allowance around the entire neckline edge to hold the facing and neckline insert in place.

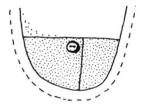

FIGURE 13. Add a button to the insert overlap.

Another option for the insert pieces is to sew in a zipper, using the technique described on page 11 (Fig. 14).

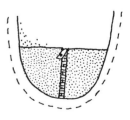

FIGURE 14. The insert can also be made with a zipper.

3

Classic Cardigans

✦ ZIP-FRONT CARDIGAN ✦

The triangles on this shirt were inspired by a hotel bellman's uniform I observed on one of my seminar trips. So, keep your eyes open; fresh ideas for these projects can be found just about anywhere!

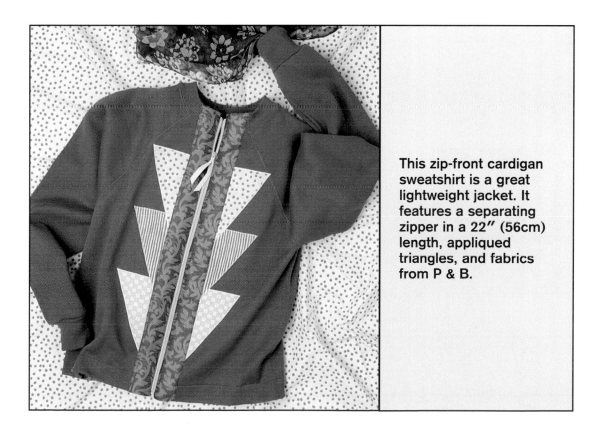

This zip-front cardigan sweatshirt is a great lightweight jacket. It features a separating zipper in a 22" (56cm) length, appliqued triangles, and fabrics from P & B.

Supplies Needed

- one sweatshirt
- ¾ yd. (68.5cm) woven fabric for zipper trim and bottom facing
- 1 yd. (91.5cm) lightweight fusible interfacing
- one separating zipper (opens and separates at the bottom) for the length of the sweatshirt front
- ¼ yd. (23cm) paper-backed fusible web
- ¼ yd. (23cm) fabric—or less—for each of the three triangle appliques (three different colors)
- 1 yd. (91.5cm) stabilizer
- 4" (10cm) ribbon or cord (optional)

➤ **Before You Begin:** In this sweatshirt project, you need to consider two things at the outset: the sweatshirt size and the separating zipper. First of all, the sweatshirt should fit well and be comfortable with the bottom ribbing removed. This alteration works best with no ribbing on the bottom of the shirt, so the front of the sweatshirt hangs straight when the shirt is worn and the zipper is open (Fig. 1).

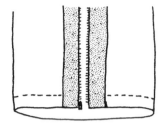

FIGURE 1. The sweatshirt fronts hang straight when the bottom ribbing is removed and the zip front alteration is added.

Second, you need to consider the length of the separating zipper. Since these zippers come only in certain lengths—18" (45.5cm), 20" (51cm), 22" (56cm), 24" (61cm)—you need to select a zipper that is closest to or slightly shorter than the length of the sweatshirt front. Slightly shorter is better than slightly longer. If the front length of your sweatshirt is 23" (58.5cm), buy a 22" (56cm) zipper and sew it to fabric strips the actual length of the sweatshirt. You'll see that it's not necessary for the zipper to be the exact length of the shirt.

1 Remove the sweatshirt bottom ribbing, using the instructions on page 7. Press the shirt's cut edges. If they are not straight or even, measure and re-cut the bottom edges as explained on page 12.

2 Measure the circumference of the bottom edge of the sweatshirt and add ½" (1.3cm) for a seam allowance.

Cut a strip of fabric to that measurement and 2½" (6.5cm) wide. Using a ¼" (6mm) seam allowance, sew the short ends of the strip together, with right sides of the fabric together. Turn ½" (1.3cm) under and press one long edge of the strip (Fig. 2).

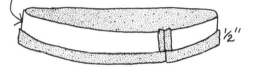

FIGURE 2. Cut and sew a strip of fabric 2½" wide, turn under a ½" hem and the hem facing is ready to sew to the sweatshirt.

This will become the upper edge of the hem facing. Pin the unpressed edge of the facing strip to the shirt, right sides of fabrics together, and sew around the shirt with a ¼" (6mm) seam allowance. Press and turn the facing to the inside of the shirt, press again, and pin. Sew the folded edge of the facing to the shirt, making sure that the bobbin thread matches the sweatshirt color, unless you want an obvious seam on the right side of the shirt (Fig. 3).

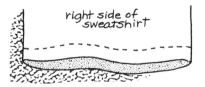

FIGURE 3. Topstitch the hem facing in place.

3 Now we're ready to begin working with the zipper and making the sweatshirt into a cardigan. With a chalk marker or a washable marking pen, mark the entire length of center front on the sweatshirt, using the instructions on page 5 to guide you. Measure the length of the center front line.

4 Because it's much easier and less frustrating to sew the firm edges of a zipper to woven fabric instead of to the knit fabric edges of the sweatshirt, cut two pieces of fabric 4" (10cm) wide and 4" (10cm) longer than the center front measurement. If the fabric strips are soft or if you want to give them more stability, fuse them with lightweight interfacing. You can fuse the entire strip or half of it, depending on how stable you want the fabric to be (Fig. 4).

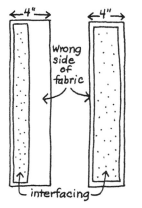

FIGURE 4. Fuse interfacing to the entire width or only half the width of the fabric strips for the zipper unit.

5 Sew the strips by folding the fabric in half with right sides together. Sew down the cut edges on the side and across the bottom. Clip the seam allowances and corners and turn the fabric right side out (Fig. 5).

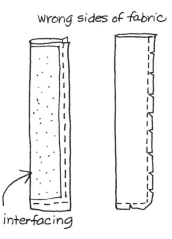

FIGURE 5. Sew the fabric strips together, wrong sides out, clip and trim the corners, and turn the strips right side out.

6 Take the zipper out of its package and press it flat before sewing on it. I've found that zippers develop permanent crease marks in their packages that are impossible to remove once you have sewn them to the fabric. A word of caution about pressing separating zippers: If they have metal teeth, they'll get hot from the pressing, so watch your fingers. (Can you tell I've learned this from experience?)

7 Line up the bottom end of the zipper with the sewn ends of the fabric strips. Place the seam side of the strips next to the zipper teeth (Fig. 6). Pin the zipper to the strips. At the top of the zipper tape you will find plastic coated ends. You can cut these off and turn under the zipper tape (Fig. 7). Sew the zipper to the fabric pieces, sewing from the bottom edge to the top. Do not sew past the top edge of the zipper tape. Set the zipper unit aside while you plan and sew the appliques to the shirt front.

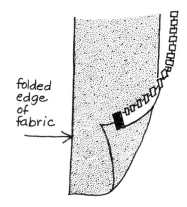

FIGURE 6. Place zipper bottom end at the stitched end of the fabric strip.

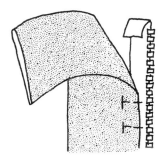

FIGURE 7. Pin the zipper to the fabric strips and turn under the zipper tape at the top.

8 Trace the Triangle Pattern on page 47 onto a folded piece of paper (Fig. 8) and cut it out. Then, on paper-backed fusible web, trace three triangles. Fuse each one to the wrong side of a different color fabric, and cut it out.

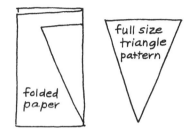

FIGURE 8. Make a full size triangle pattern by tracing the pattern from the book on folded paper.

9 Arrange the triangles on the shirt front, using the photograph as a guide. Place the zipper unit over the top, centered on the sweatshirt to test the arrangement of the triangles. To move the triangles farther apart, cut each one in half along the center line and place them 1″ (2.5cm) away from the center front line of the shirt (Fig. 9). Fuse them in place.

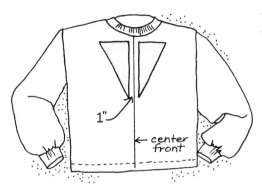

FIGURE 9. To show more of the triangle fabrics, cut each triangle in half and place them 1″ away from the center front line. Fuse in place.

10 Lay the zipper unit on top of the triangles and mark the edges on the triangles (Fig. 10). This will be a guide for your stitching.

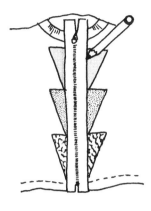

FIGURE 10. Trace the edges of the zipper unit on the triangles to use as a guide for stitching the triangles in place.

11 Before sewing the edges of the triangle appliques, place a large piece of stabilizer under the sweatshirt front. I chose a traditional applique satin stitch (see page 73 for machine applique instructions) and sewed slightly past the markings to make sure the zipper unit would cover the applique stitches (Fig. 11). Remove the stabilizer.

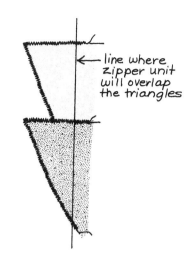

FIGURE 11. Satin stitch slightly past the line of the zipper unit placement.

12 Carefully pin the zipper unit to the center front of the shirt, using many pins. The bottom of the unit will line up with the sweatshirt bottom (Fig. 12). At the top there will be extra fabric extending over the ribbing.

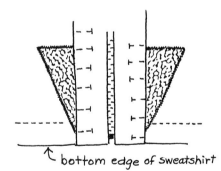

FIGURE 12. Use plenty of pins to hold the zipper unit to the sweatshirt. Line up the bottoms of the shirt and the zipper unit.

13 Sew the outside edges of the zipper unit to the sweatshirt, stitching from the bottom to the neck edge. Stop sewing ½″ (1.3cm) from the top of the neck ribbing. Sew a second row of stitching ¼″ (6mm) away from the first row. Turn the sweatshirt wrong side out and cut away the shirt fabric between the stitching lines on the zipper unit sides (Fig. 13).

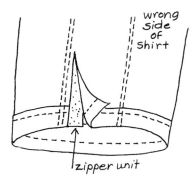

FIGURE 13. On the wrong side of the shirt, cut away the sweatshirt fabric between the stitching lines that attached the zipper unit to the front of the shirt.

14 Trim the excess fabric from the tops of the fabric strips and turn the edges inside, lining up the fabric ends with the top of the ribbing (Fig. 14). Sew across the fabric strip ends.

FIGURE 14. Trim off extra fabric at the top of the zipper unit and turn edges inside, level with the top of the ribbing before stitching across.

15 To make it easier to open and close the zipper, tie a piece of narrow ribbon, cord, or a classy tassel to the zipper pull.

I hope you'll enjoy sewing and wearing this shirt. It's the easiest way I've found to make a zip-front opening.

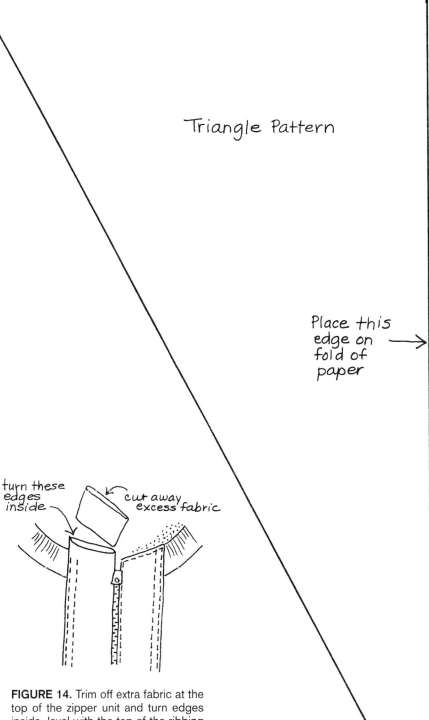

Triangle Pattern

Place this edge on fold of paper →

✦ BANDED CARDIGAN ✦ WITH MATCHING RIBBING

It may come as a surprise to you that the wide ribbing you remove from the bottom of the sweatshirt yields enough fabric to make a narrow ribbing band around the neckline and front of a cardigan sweatshirt. I've found the "self-rib" to be a nice, subtle trim.

Open a sweatshirt front and add sew-on bands of ribbing to finish the edges. You can use the sweatshirt's bottom ribbing, as I've shown on the pink shirt, or you can use a contrast color ribbing and then add more to the bottom hem and sleeves, as I've shown on the teal shirt. I've also added bias trim around the panel and applique shapes and closures of Ultrasuede to the front for a more interesting look.

Supplies Needed

- one sweatshirt
- ⅛ yd. (11.5cm) for hem facing
- ¼ yd. (23cm) ribbing or the wide ribbing from sweatshirt bottom edge

1 Remove the bottom ribbing from the sweatshirt and straighten the hem edge, using the instructions on pages 7 and 12. Even if you have chosen to use other ribbing, it's a good idea to make a straight, non-rib facing on the bottom of the sweatshirt to avoid the problem I call "cardigan bottom curve syndrome" (Fig. 1).

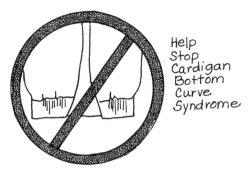

FIGURE 1. By removing the sweatshirt's bottom ribbing, you'll be able to prevent the bottom of the cardigan from curving away from the center front.

3 With a chalk marker or washable marking pen, mark the center front line of the sweatshirt, using the directions on page 5. Trace the Neckline Curve Template from the book (Fig. 3) onto a piece of paper, cut it out, and place it on the sweatshirt neckline (Fig. 4). Trace the edges of the template onto the shirt to set the curved neck edges of the cardigan front.

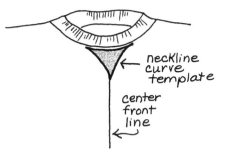

FIGURE 4. Trace the neckline curve template at the center front of the sweatshirt neckline.

2 You'll need to make and sew on the hem facing before proceeding with the cardigan banding. Measure the circumference of the bottom edge of the sweatshirt and add ½″ (1.3cm). Using this measurement for the length and 2″ (5cm) for the width, cut a strip of fabric for the hem facing. Then, refer to the instructions on page 10 for sewing on the facing. After attaching and topstitching the hem facing, the sweatshirt is ready to be turned into a cardigan (Fig. 2).

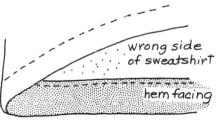

FIGURE 2. Add a hem facing to the bottom edge of the sweatshirt after removing the ribbing.

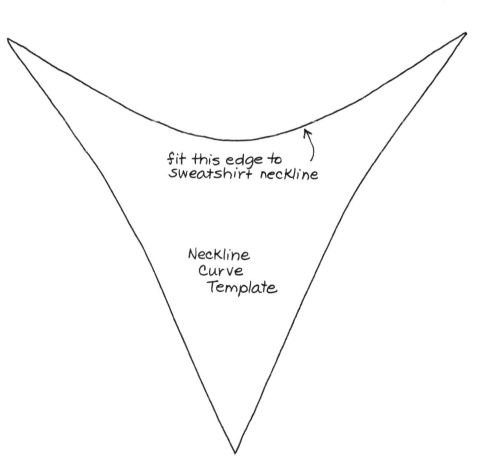

FIGURE 3. Neckline curve template.

4 Staystitch ⅛″ (3mm) from the edge on each side of the center front line, using the instructions on page 7. Begin sewing at the bottom of the shirt and sew on the neckline curve lines, around the back of the neck, and down the other side of the shirt front. Cut on the center front line and also cut away the neck ribbing to make the front opening in the cardigan (Fig. 5).

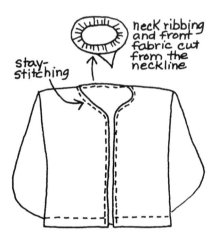

FIGURE 5. Staystitch on each side of the center front line and around the neck before cutting the shirt front open.

5 Turn back to the piece of ribbing you cut off the bottom of the shirt. Cut the circle of ribbing open and press

the cut edges flat. Cut the ribbing strip in half along the fold. Sew the two long ribbing strips together at the short ends (Fig. 6).

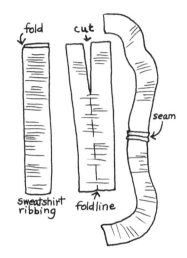

FIGURE 6. Cut the sweatshirt bottom ribbing in half on the foldline and then sew the two pieces together end to end.

6 With wrong sides of the fabric together, fold and press the long ribbing strip in half, meeting the cut edges (Fig. 7).

FIGURE 7. Fold and press the ribbing in half.

7 To apply the ribbing to the shirt, follow the procedure I learned from Sandra Betzina Webster's book *More Power Sewing:* Measure from shoulder to shoulder on the back neck edge using the edge of the tape measure. Take ⅔ of this measurement and fit this amount of ribbing between the shoulders. For example, if the measure is 9″ (23cm), then 6″ (15cm) is the length of ribbing to fit to the back neckline. With a chalk marker or a washable marking pen, mark the ⅔ measure on the cut edges of the ribbing, with the center of the measurement at the seamline of the ribbing. Meet the seamline of the strip of ribbing and the center back of the neckline, with right sides of the fabrics together (Fig. 8). Stretch and pin the ribbing marks to the shoulders of the sweatshirt. Fit and pin the ribbing to the back neckline.

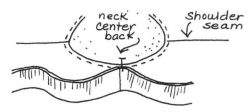

FIGURE 8. Begin pinning the ribbing to the neckline by meeting the seamline on the ribbing to the shirt's center back.

8 Next, measure from the shoulder along the edge to the center bottom of the shirt front (Fig. 9).

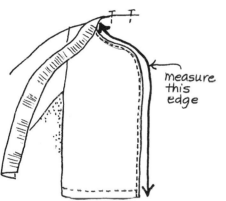

FIGURE 9. Measure from the shoulder to the bottom front edge of the shirt.

Subtract 1″ (2.5cm) from the measurement and pin this amount of ribbing to the sweatshirt. At the point where the ribbing band will end at the bottom edge of the sweatshirt, turn the ribbing right sides together and sew across the end. Trim away the excess ribbing and turn the ribbing right side out (Fig. 10). Pin the ribbing to both front edges of the sweatshirt, and sew or serge with a ¼″ (6mm) seam allowance.

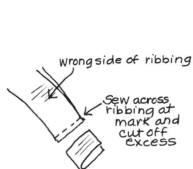

FIGURE 10. Mark the place where the ribbing and the bottom edge of the sweatshirt meet, turn the ribbing wrong sides out to sew across at the mark, and then trim off the extra ribbing.

9 Press the seam and then press the seam allowances toward the shirt. Understitch to secure the ribbing band and shirt seam allowances to the shirt, using the directions on page 10.

This cardigan does not use any closures but is simply an open jacket. If you are interested in adding a closure, see Banded Cardigan with Contrast Ribbing on page 55.

✦ Banded Cardigan ✦ with Contrast Ribbing

This cardigan variation (see photo on page 48) features contrast color ribbing around the edges and front panel trim—a slightly more dramatic change than the Banded Cardigan with Matching Ribbing. Note the pointed hemline in front and back.

Supplies Needed

- one sweatshirt with set-in sleeves

- ½ yd. (46cm) paper-backed fusible web

- ½ yd. (46cm) fabric for front panel

- 1 yd. (91.5cm) bias tape or ½ yd. (46cm) fabric to make your own

- ½ yd. (46cm) ribbing

- 24" (61cm) of narrow ribbon, cord, or Ultrasuede strip for closures

- two buttons

- ¼ yd. (23cm) paper-backed fusible web (optional)

- small pieces of Ultrasuede (optional)

- ½ yd. (46cm) stabilizer (optional)

1 Remove the bottom ribbing from the sweatshirt, using the instructions on page 7. Press the shirt's cut edges. If they are not straight or even, measure and re-cut the bottom edges, as explained on page 12. Using a chalk marker or a washable marking pen, mark the center front line on the sweatshirt, using the instructions on page 5 as a guide. Trace the Neckline Curve Template from Figure 3 on page 49 and use it to draw the new cardigan neckline at center front (Fig. 4 on page 49).

2 Staystitch ⅛" (3mm) on one side of the center front line, continuing on and around the curved neckline, and back down the other side of the center front line to the bottom of the shirt. Cut away only the neck ribbing and the fabric inside the neckline (Fig. 1).

3 To make the front fabric panel, cut a piece of paper-backed fusible web 11" × 13" (28 × 33cm). Fold the paper in quarters and cut to round out the corners (Fig. 2). Fuse the paper to the wrong side of the fabric you've chosen for the front panel and cut out the shape, cutting the edge off the paper-backed fusible web. Remove the paper backing.

FIGURE 2. Trim to round the corners on a 11" × 13" piece of paper-backed fusible web.

FIGURE 1. After staystitching on each side of the center front line and around the neck on the template lines, cut away only the ribbing and fabric inside the template stitching lines.

4 Position the fused panel at the center front and 1" (2.5cm) from the shoulder seams (Fig. 3). Before fusing the fabric to the sweatshirt, cut away the fabric portion extending past the front neckline edge (Fig. 4).

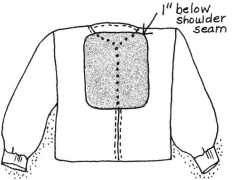

FIGURE 3. Place the fabric panel on the shirt front with the top edge 1" below the shoulder seams.

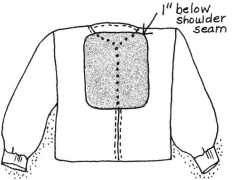

FIGURE 4. Trim away the fabric extending past the curved neckline edges.

5 Measure around the edges of the panel to determine the length of bias tape you'll need. Use purchased tape or make your own. Don't be afraid to use a contrasting print for bias. You'll often see unusual fabric mixes in ready-to-wear, so walk on the wild side and try it yourself! If there is a seam in the bias, you may want to position it at the center bottom edge of the panel so it will be covered when the cardigan band is applied (Fig. 5).

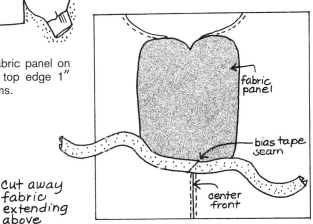

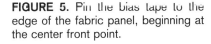

FIGURE 5. Pin the bias tape to the edge of the fabric panel, beginning at the center front point.

6 Lay the bias tape over the edge of the panel, pressing curves in place. Pin the tape to the shirt and then sew around it. Sew the inside edge first and then the outside edge (Fig. 6).

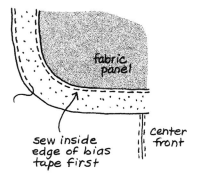

FIGURE 6. Sew the bias tape to the sweatshirt. Stitch the inside edge first.

7 Next, cut the new hemline for the sweatshirt. On each side fold of the shirt, measure 3" (7.5cm) up from the bottom edge, and mark that point with a chalk marker or washable marking pen. Draw a straight line from each mark to the bottom of the center front line (Fig. 7). Cut along the lines, cutting both the front and back of the shirt.

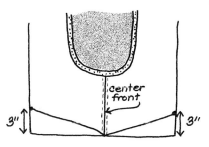

FIGURE 7. Cut a new hemline for the front and back of the sweatshirt by cutting from 3" on the shirt sides to the center front line.

8 Turn to the wrong side of the shirt front and cut between the staystitching lines up the center front to turn the sweatshirt into a cardigan. (Fig. 8).

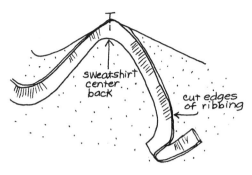

FIGURE 9. Begin pinning the ribbing to the sweatshirt bottom edge at the center back.

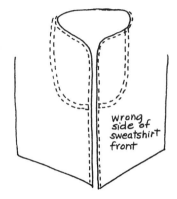

FIGURE 8. On the wrong side of the shirt front, cut open the sweatshirt between the two staystitching lines.

9 Measure the distance around the bottom edge of the shirt. Cut a 2″ (5cm) strip of ribbing (you'll need to piece this strip) 1″ (2.5cm) shorter than the actual measurement. Fold and press the ribbing in half with wrong sides together, meeting the raw edges. Mark the center of the strip and meet it to the center back of the shirt (Fig. 9). Adjust and pin the ribbing to the entire bottom edge. Sew or serge the ribbing on with a ¼″ (6mm) seam allowance. Press the seam, turn the seam allowance toward the shirt, and understitch, using the instructions on page 10.

10 Fit and sew the ribbing band to the front and neckline edges of the shirt, referring to Steps 7 and 8 of Ribbing Banded Cardigan on page 50. This 2″ (5cm) ribbing band should also be understitched so the seam allowances are attached to the shirt.

11 To determine the length of the new sleeve treatment, try on the shirt. With a pin, chalk marker, or washable marking pen, mark where you want to cut off the cuff and a portion of the sleeve (Fig. 10).

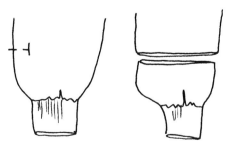

FIGURE 10. Mark and cut the sleeves.

Cut 2″ (5cm) wide ribbing strips for each sleeve. Measure the sleeve ends and cut a piece of ribbing ½″ (1.3cm) less than the measurement. Sew the ends of the ribbing together to make a circle, press the seam, and fold the ribbing in half with wrong sides together, meeting the raw edges (Fig. 11). Pin the ribbing to the sleeve end, meeting right sides of the fabric. Sew with a ¼″ (6mm) seam allowance and press. Turn the band down to form the end of the sleeve. Understitch the seam allowances to the sweatshirt, using the instructions on page 10 (Fig. 12).

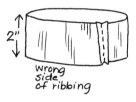

FIGURE 11. Cut and sew ribbing for the sleeve ends.

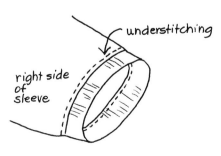

FIGURE 12. Sew the ribbing band to the sleeve end. Understitch the seam allowance to the sweatshirt.

12 For the closures on this cardigan, cut two narrow 12″ (30.5cm) strips of ribbon, cord, or Ultrasuede. Knot the ends of each strip. Fold the strip in half and cross the strip to form a loop to fit over the buttons you've chosen for this cardigan (Fig. 13). Pin the looped strips to the cardigan front. Cut two non-fray fabric pieces ½″ × 1″ (1.3 × 2.5cm). Place and sew these over the crossing of the strips (Fig. 14). Pin or sew the buttons to the other side of the cardigan front.

13 Appliques are optional. I used 1″ (2.5cm) squares and lightning bolts cut from Ultrasuede to decorate my cardigan. Trace the Square and Lightning Appliques from the book (Fig. 15) onto paper-backed fusible web. Fuse them to the sweatshirt with the traditional applique method (see page 73), remembering to cover the Ultrasuede pieces with a press cloth before fusing, or pin or tape the pieces to the sweatshirt.

➤**Applique Note:** In the area of the fabric panel, the sweatshirt is very stable, but if you place the applique shapes outside of the panel, as I did with some of them, be sure to place stabilizer on the back of the sweatshirt before sewing. For nearly invisible stitching, use clear nylon thread and a very small zigzag or buttonhole stitch on the appliques.

This version of a cardigan is a creative sweatshirt with lots of style. Enjoy making it and wearing it. Get ready for lots of compliments.

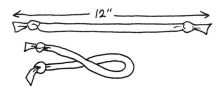

FIGURE 13. Knot the ends of a 12″ strip of fabric or ribbon and fold the strip in half to form a loop.

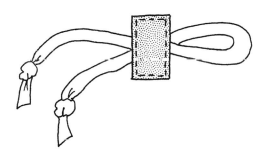

FIGURE 14. Sew a ½″ × 1″ piece of non-fray fabric over the crossed strips forming the loop.

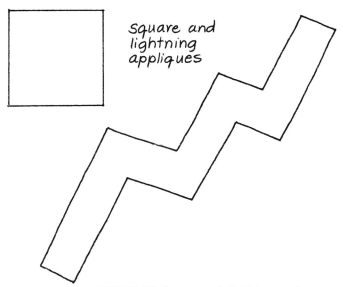

square and lightning appliques

FIGURE 15. Square and lightning appliques.

Creative Cuffs, Sleeves, Pockets, & Hems

4

✦ REPLACEMENT SLEEVE CUFFS ✦

You can renew a sweatshirt with cuffs that have become stained or worn by replacing the sleeve cuffs. If the polo collar is sized for an adult, you might be able to get both cuffs from one collar; otherwise plan to have two collars for this project.

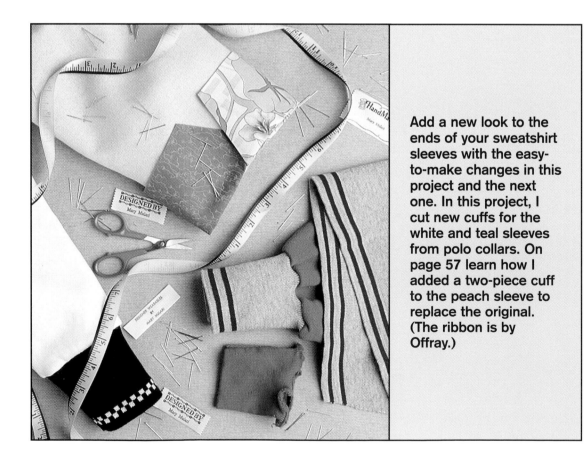

Add a new look to the ends of your sweatshirt sleeves with the easy-to-make changes in this project and the next one. In this project, I cut new cuffs for the white and teal sleeves from polo collars. On page 57 learn how I added a two-piece cuff to the peach sleeve to replace the original. (The ribbon is by Offray.)

Supplies Needed

- one sweatshirt
- one or two polo/finished-edge knit collars

1 Remove the sleeve cuffs from the sweatshirt, using the instructions for removing ribbing on page 7. Save the original cuffs to use as a guide for sizing the new cuffs.

2 Measure the folded edge of the original cuffs and add ½" (1.3cm) to the measurement for seam allowances. Using a chalk marker or a washable marking pen, mark the measurement on the finished edge of the collar. If you have enough collar fabric, draw a tapered line to the collar's raw edge (Fig. 1). Also, check the raw edge. If it is raveling or thick, trim away the edge so the end of the collar is flat.

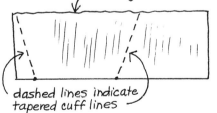

FIGURE 1. Measure the cuff circumference on the finished edge of the collar. Draw tapered lines to the raw edge of the collar.

3 Cut the cuffs from the collars. With the right sides of the fabric together, sew the cuff sides together using a ¼" (6mm) seam allowance. Try on the cuffs to make sure they fit.

4 Mark the quarter portions on each sleeve end and each cuff, as explained on page 8. For each cuff: Match up the marks on the right side of the new cuff and the right side of sleeve and pin the marks together. You may have to do some serious stretching, but the cuff and the sleeve will fit together (Fig. 2).

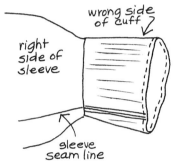

FIGURE 2. With the right side of the cuff to the right side of the sleeve, line up the seamlines of the cuff and sleeve before sewing or serging the cuff and sleeve ends together.

5 Sew or serge each cuff to its sleeve with a ¼" (6mm) seam allowance.

Unique polo collars with patterns or designs look great on cuffs as well as necklines. If you have an extra collar, add it to the neckline with the method shown in Some Bunny Sweatshirt on page 125.

TWO-PIECE CUFFS

Change a sweatshirt's style by removing the original sleeve cuffs and part of the sleeves. Choose two coordinating fabrics to make two-piece cuffs. You can apply a similar style to the bottom of the sweatshirt by following the instructions for the Two-Piece Tunic Extension on page 68.

Supplies Needed

- one sweatshirt
- ¼ yd. (23cm) of two fabrics

1 Try on the sweatshirt to plan the new sleeve length and cuff location. Mark the end of the new sleeve with pins and take off the shirt.

2 Align the two ends of the sleeves, pin them together, and cut off both sleeves at the same time (Fig. 1).

FIGURE 1. Cut the ends off both sleeves.

With the sleeves flat on a table, measure across the cut-off edge and add 2″ (5cm). For example, the sleeves on the sweatshirt illustrated measured 6½″ (16.5cm), so I cut half of the cuff 8½″ (22cm) long. For each sleeve, cut two pieces of fabric to the measurement and 7″ (18cm) wide (Fig. 2).

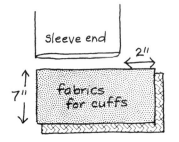

FIGURE 2. Add 2″ to the measurement across the sleeve ends and cut two cuff fabrics to that measure and 7″ wide.

3 To join the two fabric pieces for each cuff, place the right side of the fabric together and sew along the 7″ (18cm) edge with a ¼″ (6mm) seam allowance (Fig. 3). Press the seam.

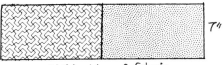

FIGURE 3. Sew the two cuff fabrics together.

4 Fold the joined fabrics horizontally in the center with right sides together. On the folded edge, using a chalk marker or a washable marking

pen, mark points 1½″ (4cm) from each edge. (Fig. 4). Sew from the point you marked to the corner. Trim and clip the seam allowance, press, and turn the cuff right side out. (Fig. 5).

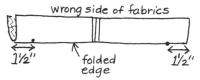

FIGURE 4. Fold the fabric in half with right sides together and mark 1½″ in from each end.

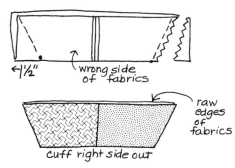

FIGURE 5. Sew from the 1½″ points to the corner of each end.

5 Before pinning and sewing the cuff to the sleeve, plan which fabric you want to have overlapping the other. Place the cuff inside the sweatshirt sleeve, and pin the seamline of the cuff to the seamline of the sleeve (Fig. 6). Continue pinning the cuff around the sleeve and overlap the two ends.

6 Sew or serge the cuff to the shirt. (You'll appreciate the open arm of your sewing machine here.) Press. Turn the cuff to the outside of the sleeve and press again (Fig. 7).

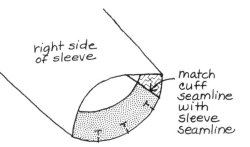

FIGURE 6. Pin the cuff inside the sleeve, matching the seamlines of the cuff and sleeve.

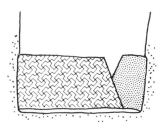

FIGURE 7. After sewing the cuff to the sleeve, turn it to the outside of the sleeve and press it.

7 To secure the cuff to the seamline and to help keep it in place, stitch in the seamline "ditch" (Fig. 8).

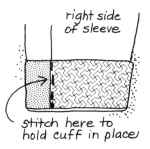

FIGURE 8. Stitch over the seamline of the cuff and sleeve to secure the cuff.

I like to use two different fabrics for this cuff alteration, but using one fabric would work just as well, plus you would eliminate the step of sewing the two fabric pieces together.

✦ SLEEVE-GATHERING TRIM ✦

For this sleeve-shortening addition, I recommend selecting cord, ribbon, or fabric that is not slippery. That way the bows and knots you tie to gather the sleeves won't easily slip open.

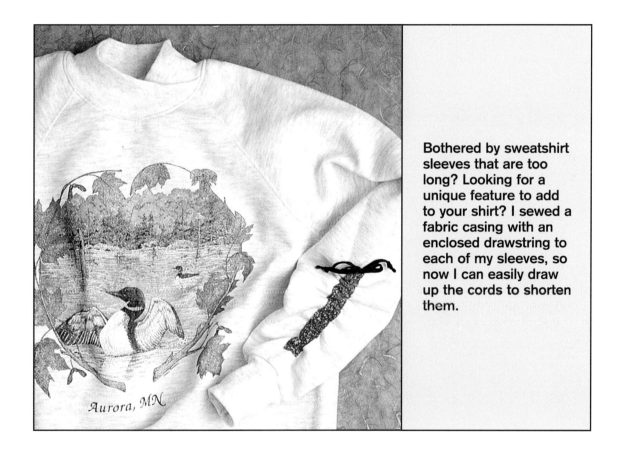

Bothered by sweatshirt sleeves that are too long? Looking for a unique feature to add to your shirt? I sewed a fabric casing with an enclosed drawstring to each of my sleeves, so now I can easily draw up the cords to shorten them.

 ## Supplies Needed

- one sweatshirt with long sleeves

- ⅛ yd. (11.5cm) fabric for casing

- 48″ (120cm) cord, ribbon, or Ultrasuede

1 Using a seam ripper, cut the sleeve seam open from the cuff end to about 8″ (18cm) up the sleeve (Fig. 1). This will make it easier for you to sew the gathering piece onto the sleeve.

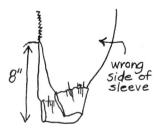

FIGURE 1. Open the sleeve seam 8″ to make it easier to add the gathering system.

2 Cut two 9" x 1½" (23 x 4cm) strips of fabric. Turn under and press ¼" (6mm) seam allowances on the long sides and ½" (1.3cm) on the short ends (Fig. 2).

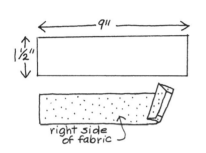

FIGURE 2. Turn under and press the seam allowances.

3 Cut two 24" (61cm) strips of cord or ribbon, or make narrow fabric ties. Taking one fabric strip and one cord, pin both ends of the cord to one end of the wrong side of the fabric, inside the seam allowance. Pin at intervals to keep the cord in the center of the casing while you are sewing. Keep all pins on the right side of the fabric (Fig. 3). Do the same with the remaining cord and fabric strip.

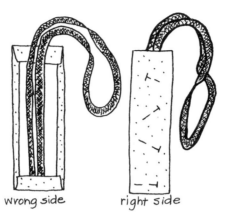

FIGURE 3. Pin the cords onto the fabric casings. Keep all the pins on the right side of the fabric.

4 Pin the casings to the sleeves on the center fold line, about 1½" (4cm) above the ribbing. Leaving just enough room for the cords to come out of the casing, sew on the top and sides of the casing and back and forth at two places across the bottom to secure the cord ends (Fig. 4).

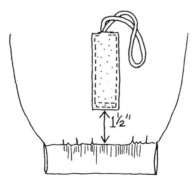

FIGURE 4. Sew around the casing, leaving just enough room for the cords to come out of the top.

5 Cut the loose end of the cords in two, knot the ends, and tie in a bow or knot to gather up the sleeves (Fig. 5). Sew or serge the sleeve seams closed.

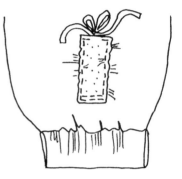

FIGURE 5. Cut the cord ends and tie in a bow to gather the sleeves.

Consider using different fabrics and ties on each sleeve. After all, only tradition says our sleeves must look identical. Then, use some or all of the same fabric to trim other areas of the shirt. I used mine to add Hem Facing with Shirt Tails (page 64).

✦ ZIPPERED SLEEVE POCKETS ✦

Add this decorative pocket for looks or usefulness. If you're right handed, you'll appreciate the pocket most if it is sewn to the left sleeve of the sweatshirt.

A pocket on the sleeve opposite your dominant hand can be a small, handy storage space for coins, a key, or other necessities. On this shirt, I sewed a zipper frame to attach to the sleeve, with the pocket inside.

Supplies Needed

- one sweatshirt
- small pieces of fabric for zipper edges and pocket backing
- one 7" (18cm) or shorter zipper
- 4" (10cm) cord or ribbon (optional)

1 Turn the sleeve of the sweatshirt inside out. Use a seam ripper to cut the sleeve seam open from the cuff end to about 10" (25.5cm) or so up the sleeve (Fig. 1). This will make it easier for you to insert the pocket addition without struggling.

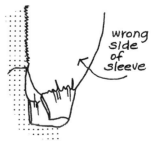

wrong side of sleeve

FIGURE 1. Undo the stitching to open up the sleeve seam, about 10".

2 Cut two 1¼″ (3cm) wide strips of fabric as long as the zipper opening will be. Turn under ¼″ (6mm) and press both edges of both strips. Sew them to the zipper sides (Fig. 2).

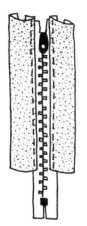

FIGURE 2. Sew fabric strips to the zipper sides.

Cut two 2½″ (6.5cm) squares of fabric, one for each zipper end. Turn under and press the edges to line up with the zipper unit. Sew the fabric pieces over the zipper ends, shortening the zipper if you wish; the shirt illustrated has a 4″ (10cm) zipper. Cut away the excess zipper length (Fig. 3).

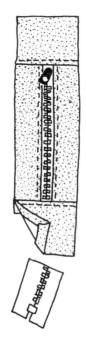

FIGURE 3. Cut away any extra zipper length after sewing the fabric ends to "frame" the zipper.

3 Pin the zipper unit over the center folded edge of the sleeve about 2″ (5cm) from the ribbing (Fig. 4).

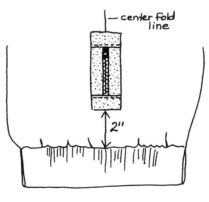

FIGURE 4. Place and pin the zipper on the sleeve center foldline about 2″ from the top of the ribbing.

Sew around the edges to secure the unit to the shirt. On the inside of the sleeve, cut away the fabric inside the stitching, leaving ½″ (1.3cm) of fabric around inside the stitching (Fig. 5).

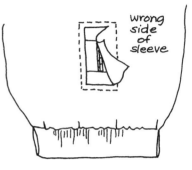

FIGURE 5. Cut away the fabric between the stitching lines, leaving a ½″ seam allowance.

4 Measure the zipper unit length and the distance to the cut edge of the sweatshirt sleeve (Fig. 6). Cut a piece of fabric slightly larger than the measurements. Zigzag or serge the edges.

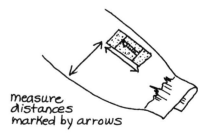

FIGURE 6. To determine the size of the back pocket fabric, measure the zipper unit length and the distance to the edge of the sleeve.

5 Place the fabric inside the sleeve, right side of the fabric to the wrong side of the sweatshirt (Fig. 7).

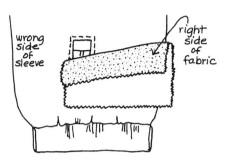

FIGURE 7. Place the pocket fabric inside the sleeve over the zipper unit stitching and over the side seam allowance of the sleeve.

Carefully pin it over the zipper unit stitching and over the cut edge of the sleeve seam allowance. Because the fabric piece is larger than the zipper unit and area to the sleeve edge, it won't be difficult to sew from the right side of the shirt to form the pocket on the inside of

the sleeve. Stitch from the sleeve edge, across the top edge of the zipper unit, and back down to the sleeve edge (Fig. 8). Use thread to match the sweatshirt color so the stitching line will not be obvious.

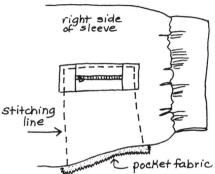

FIGURE 8. Sew along the sides and across the top of the zipper unit to secure the pocket lining to the sleeve.

6 With the right sides of the sleeve together, resew or serge the sleeve seam back together. Trim off the excess

pocket lining in the process of serging or cut it off after sewing (Fig. 9).

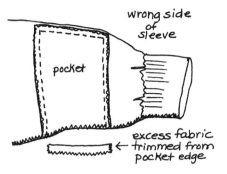

FIGURE 9. Sew or serge the sleeve seam together and trim off the extra pocket fabric.

7 Tie a small piece of cord or ribbon to the zipper pull to make it easier to open and close the zipper.

For a finishing touch, coordinate the zipper trim with other decorations on the shirt. My suggestion: Change the original neckline by adding a Zipper Collar, using the instructions on page 13.

✦ HEM FACING WITH SHIRTTAILS ✦

This sweatshirt is one from my home town, and it features a design of the loon, the Minnesota state bird. The alteration provides more room at the hipline and offers a change from the band of ribbing that normally finishes the bottom edge of a sweatshirt (Fig. 1).

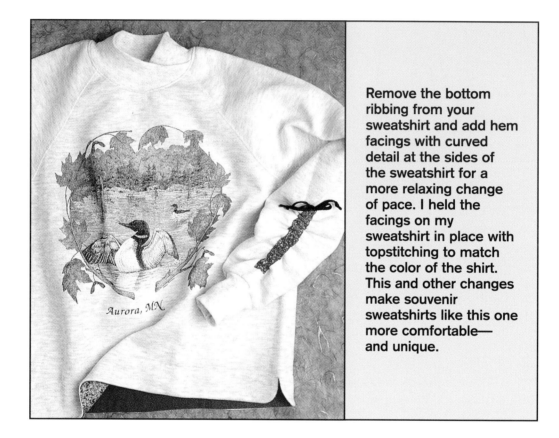

Remove the bottom ribbing from your sweatshirt and add hem facings with curved detail at the sides of the sweatshirt for a more relaxing change of pace. I held the facings on my sweatshirt in place with topstitching to match the color of the shirt. This and other changes make souvenir sweatshirts like this one more comfortable— and unique.

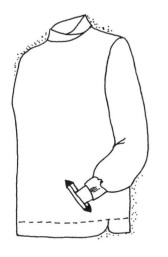

FIGURE 1. A new hemline with curved shirttails.

Supplies Needed

- one sweatshirt
- ¼ yd. (23cm) fabric for facings

1 Remove the bottom ribbing of the sweatshirt, using the instructions on page 7. Press the bottom edge and make sure it is straight. I have found that many sweatshirts have wavy edges that need to be straightened. Refer to page 12 for directions on how to fix an uneven hem edge.

2 Measure around the bottom edge of the sweatshirt and cut a piece of fabric 1" (2.5cm) longer than the measurement and 3" (7.5cm) wide. Turn under and press ½" (1.3cm) on one long edge of the fabric strip (Fig. 2). Draw lines to mark the sides of the sweatshirt about 4" (10cm) up from the bottom edge (Fig. 3).

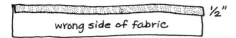

FIGURE 2. Press under ½" on one long edge of the hem facing fabric.

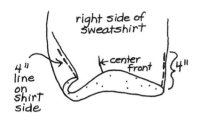

FIGURE 3. Mark the sides of the sweatshirt 4" up from the bottom edge.

3 Pin the unpressed edge of the strip with the right side of the fabric to the right side of the shirt (Fig. 4). Plan that the fabric strip ends will overlap on the front or back of the shirt but not at the sides.

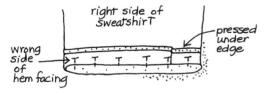

FIGURE 4. Pin the facing to the sweatshirt bottom edge, right sides facing.

4 Trace the Curved Hem Template from the book (Fig. 5) onto a piece of paper and cut it out. Trace the curved shaping on the wrong sides of the facing at the shirt sides—or at other locations, if you prefer (Fig. 6).

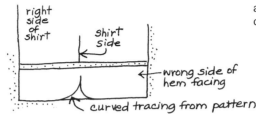

FIGURE 6. Trace the curved hem template at the side marks on each side of the shirt, drawing with a washable marking pen.

Stitch with a ¼" (6mm) seam allowance around the bottom edges of the facing and shirt to attach the facing. Sew on the lines of the curves at the shirt sides. At the top of the curves, stitch across *one* stitch instead of sewing straight up and directly down (Fig. 7). This will give the facing a smoother appearance as it folds over to the wrong side of the shirt.

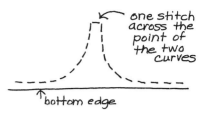

FIGURE 7. Sew up to the point of the curve, then stitch one stitch straight across before stitching the second curve.

5 Turn under and press the facing on the wrong side of the shirt. Pin it in place. Sew around the folded-under top edge of the facing to secure it to the sweatshirt (Fig. 8).

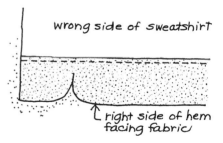

FIGURE 8. Sew the top edge of the facing to the wrong side of the sweatshirt.

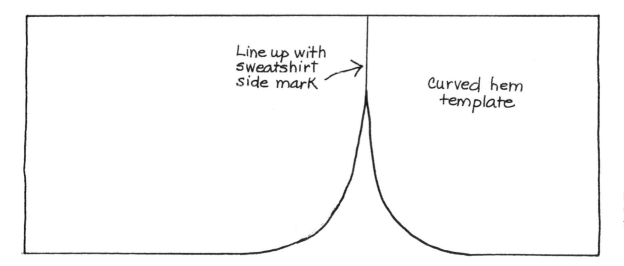

FIGURE 5. Curved hem template.

✦ TUNIC EXTENSION WITH ZIPPER ✦

This sweatshirt detail appears below the waistline for a subtle effect. Wear the zipper open or closed for different looks.

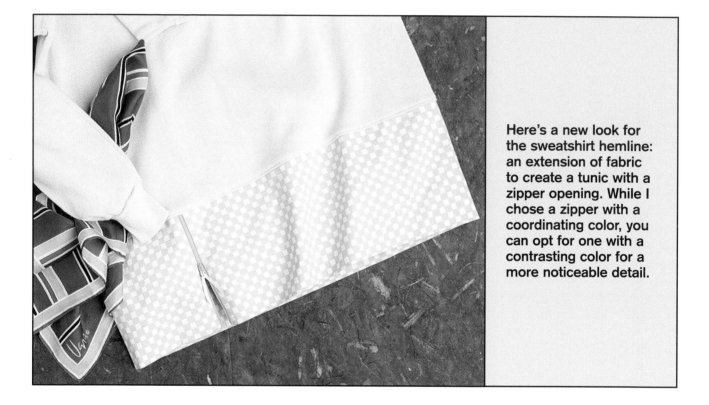

Here's a new look for the sweatshirt hemline: an extension of fabric to create a tunic with a zipper opening. While I chose a zipper with a coordinating color, you can opt for one with a contrasting color for a more noticeable detail.

 ## Supplies Needed

- one sweatshirt
- 1 yd. (91.5cm) fabric
- one 9" (23cm) or longer zipper
- 4" (10cm) cord or ribbon (optional)

1 First, remove the bottom ribbing from the sweatshirt, using the instructions on page 7. Press the bottom edge and make sure it is straight. I have found that many sweatshirts have wavy edges that need to be straightened. Refer to the instructions on page 12 to learn the best way to fix an uneven hem edge.

2 Try on the sweatshirt to determine the extra length of fabric you'll need to make it a tunic—or compare it to a tunic you like to wear. Also, check the width of the shirt to make sure that it will not be too tight in the hips if extra straight fabric pieces are added, and decide where on the sweatshirt you'd like to position the zipper opening of the extension (Fig. 1).

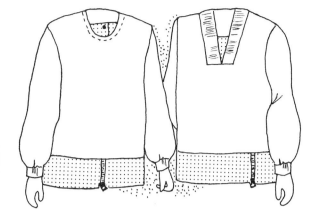

FIGURE 1. Tunic extensions with centered zipper and off-center zipper.

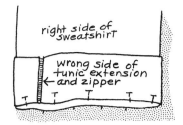

FIGURE 4. Pin the zipper extension to the shirt bottom edge, meeting the right sides of the sweatshirt and the extension.

3 With the sweatshirt back on the worktable, measure around the bottom edge. Add 1½" (4cm) to the measurement and cut a piece of fabric to that measure and *twice* the amount you want to extend the sweatshirt length. I chose to make the sweatshirt in the illustration 7" (18cm) longer, which meant that my fabric piece was 14" (35.5cm) wide (Fig. 2)

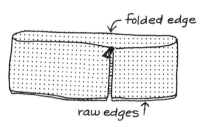

FIGURE 3. Sew the zipper to the extension fabric.

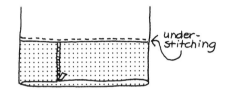

FIGURE 5. Understitch the seam allowances to the sweatshirt.

6 Wear the zipper open or partially open if you need more hip room in the tunic. Add a cord or ribbon to the zipper pull to make it easier to open or close the zipper. Another option is to sew two zippers into the tunic band, placing them at the side seams (Fig. 6).

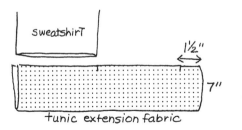

FIGURE 2. Add 1½" to the measurement of the sweatshirt bottom edge for the length of the fabric extension. The final width is 7", which requires 14" of fabric folded in half.

4 Sew the zipper to the short ends of the fabric band following the method on page 11 (Fig. 3).

5 With the right side of the tunic band facing the right side of the shirt, pin the raw edges of the fabric to the sweatshirt's bottom edge. Double-check to see that the zipper is positioned where you want it to be on the front of the sweatshirt (Fig. 4). Sew or serge around the sweatshirt with a ¼" (6mm) seam allowance, press the seam, and flip the tunic band down to become the shirt's bottom edge. Try it on to test the fit before understitching the seam allowances to the shirt, using the directions on page 10 (Fig. 5).

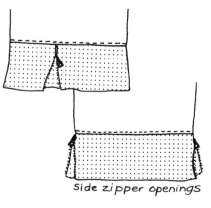

FIGURE 6. Open the zipper for more hip room in the tunic. For another option, place the zipper opening at the shirt sides.

Two-Piece Tunic Extension

Remove a sweatshirt's bottom ribbing and replace it with two coordinating fabric extensions to lengthen the shirt and turn it into a tunic. I chose two coordinating fabrics by P & B for this hemline alteration.

Supplies Needed

- one sweatshirt
- ½ yd. (46cm) of two fabrics

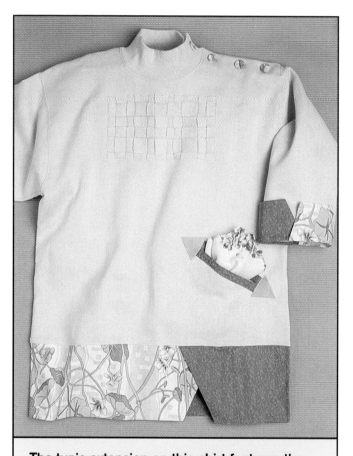

The tunic extension on this shirt features the fabrics overlapping on the shirt's right side, which allows more room in the hip area when the shirt is worn. I repeated one of the fabrics in the hidden pocket treatment (instructions on page 70), along with Ultrasuede triangles at the ends of the pocket opening. The handkerchief inside the pocket is a special one with crocheted trim by my grandmother, Ida Koski.

1 Remove the bottom ribbing from the shirt, using the instructions on page 7. Press the bottom edge and make sure it is straight. I have found that many sweatshirts have wavy edges that need to be straightened. Refer to page 12 for directions on how to fix an uneven hem edge.

2 Try on the sweatshirt to determine the extra length of fabric you'll need to make it a tunic—and compare it to a tunic you like to wear. On the sweatshirt in the illustration, I used a 6" (15cm) tunic extension (Fig. 1). Also, check the width of the shirt to make sure that it will not be too tight in the hips if extra straight fabric pieces are added.

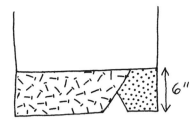

FIGURE 1. The two fabric pieces of the tunic extension add 6" of length to the sweatshirt.

3 Measure across the sweatshirt front and add 4" (10cm) to the measurement. This is the measurement to which you will cut *both* overlapping tunic sections. For example, I measured the sweatshirt in the illustration at 22" (56cm) across the front, so I cut two fabric pieces 26" (66cm) long. The width of the fabric is 12" (30.5cm) and is folded in half to make the 6" (15cm) extension (Fig. 2).

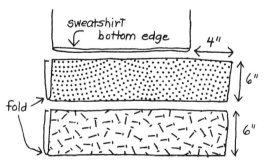

FIGURE 2. Cut the two fabrics 4" longer than the sweatshirt front measurement and 12" wide (folded up to 6").

4 Fold each fabric piece in half lengthwise, meeting right sides together. On the folded edge, using a chalk marker or washable marking pen, mark a point 3" (7.5cm) from each end. Draw lines from this point to the cut edges (Fig. 3). This will mark the stitching lines on each end of the tunic extensions. Sew along the lines, trim and clip the seam allowances, and turn the fabric pieces right side out. Press.

FIGURE 3. For each half of the extension, fold the fabric in half, meeting right sides of the fabrics. Mark 3" in from each end of the fold and draw a line to the upper corner.

5 Overlap the top, raw edges of the two fabrics 3" (7.5cm) and pin into place. Plan where the "opening" in the tunic edge will be placed on the sweatshirt. I chose to place mine on the side rather than at center front. With the front sides of the tunic extensions facing the right side of the sweatshirt, pin the raw edges together (Fig. 4). Overlap and pin the two ends on the back of the shirt. Adjust the amount of overlap on the front, if necessary. Sew or serge around the edges with a ¼" (6mm) seam allowance. Press the seam and then understitch

the seam allowances to the shirt, using the instructions on page 10 (Fig. 5).

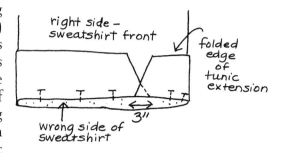

FIGURE 4. Pin the fabric extensions to the sweatshirt bottom, meeting the raw edges of the fabrics to the shirt raw edge. Overlap the two pieces 3" at both overlap locations.

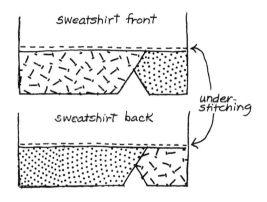

FIGURE 5. Stitch the extensions to the shirt, press the seams and understitch the seam allowances to the sweatshirt.

You'll appreciate the good looks and comfort of this new free-falling tunic extension. Consider using the same two fabrics in another area of the shirt, such as the Two-Piece Cuff alteration on page 57, or sewing a button to the overlap areas as added trim.

✦ HIDDEN SIDE POCKET ✦ WITH TRIANGLE ENDS

Add a pocket to your sweatshirt side with a classy opening for that extra special trim—and even use it to hide a few small necessities. (See the photo on page 68.)

Supplies Needed

- one sweatshirt
- ⅓ yd. (30.5cm) fabric for pocket
- 6″ (15cm) strip of tear-away stabilizer
- small scrap of Ultrasuede or other non-fray, stable fabric for triangles at pocket ends

1 Cut a 1¾″ x 12″ (4.5 x 30.5cm) strip of fabric lengthwise with the grain of fabric. Meet the raw edges with right sides of the fabric together and sew with a ¼″ (6mm) seam allowance and sew them together (Fig. 1). Turn the tube right side out.

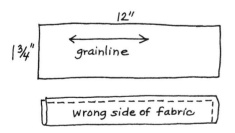

FIGURE 1. Sew a fabric tube for the pocket opening strips.

2 Press the tube, centering the seamline on the center back (Fig. 2). Cut the tube in half lengthwise and place the two 6″ (15cm) edges together

over a very narrow strip of tear-away stabilizer. Zigzag with a wide stitch between the strips with the stabilizer beneath (Fig. 3). This stitching is temporary and will be removed when the pocket is assembled.

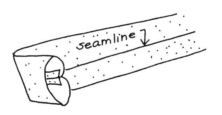

FIGURE 2. Center the seamline on the back of the fabric tube.

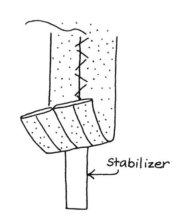

FIGURE 3. Zigzag stitch the two 6″ strips to a piece of stabilizer.

3 Try on the sweatshirt to determine the pocket location. You may even decide to make two pockets. Pin the two

strip unit to the sweatshirt where you want the pocket opening (Fig 4).

FIGURE 4. Pin the two strips to the sweatshirt in the place you want the pocket to open.

4 Cut a 7″ x 12″ (18 x 30.5cm) piece of fabric for the inside pocket lining. Zigzag or serge the edges.

5 Sew the two outer edges of the pocket opening strips to the sweatshirt (Fig. 5).

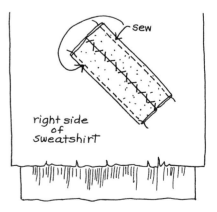

FIGURE 5. Sew along the top and bottom edges of the pocket strips to attach the unit to the sweatshirt.

On the inside of the shirt, pin one 7" (18cm) edge of the pocket lining (right side of fabric facing up) over the lower line of stitching. On the front side of the shirt and ⅛" (3mm) from the original stitching line, sew a second seam along the strip (Fig. 6).

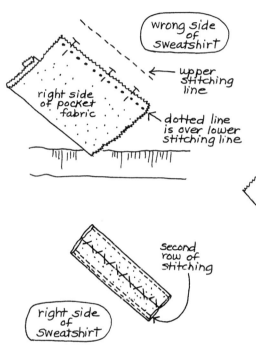

FIGURE 6. Pin the pocket lining to the wrong side of the shirt, placing one 7" edge over the lower stitching line.

6 On the wrong side of the sweatshirt, cut out the sweatshirt fleece from inside the stitching lines, leaving a ¼" (6mm) seam allowance (Fig. 7). Pin the free end of the pocket lining fabric over the stitching line on the upper edge of the pocket strip area (Fig. 8). Again, sew from the right side of the sweatshirt, sewing ⅛" (3mm) from the previous stitching line at the top edge of the strip.

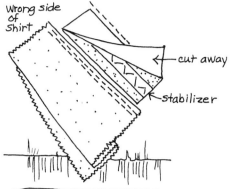

FIGURE 7. Cut away the sweatshirt fabric between the upper and lower stitching lines.

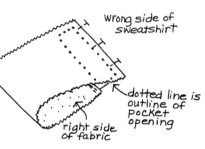

FIGURE 8. Pin the free end of the pocket lining over the upper pocket unit stitching line on the wrong side of the sweatshirt.

7 On the inside of the sweatshirt, sew together the sides of the pocket lining (Fig. 9). Pin the pocket to the sweatshirt to hold it in place while you sew on the triangle ends.

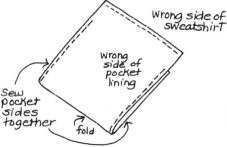

FIGURE 9. Sew the sides of the pocket lining together.

8 Trace the Triangle Pattern for Pocket Ends from the book (Fig. 10), and cut it out. Cut two triangles from Ultrasuede or other firm non-fray fabric. Place one triangle over each pocket end. First sew the side overlapping the strips, sew around, and then sew a second time over the first side you sewed (Fig. 11).

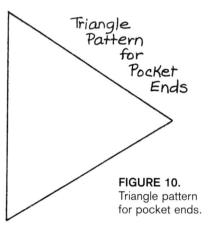

FIGURE 10. Triangle pattern for pocket ends.

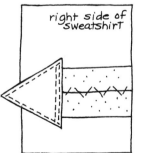

FIGURE 11. Reinforce the triangle end that overlaps the pocket opening strips.

9 Remove the zigzag basting stitch across the pocket strips and tear out the stabilizer strip.

Now, your pocket is ready for your hand, a tissue, or a little pile of money.

Too Wide Hemlines and How to Fix Them

Occasionally when sweatshirt bottom ribbings are removed, the bottom edge flares out and the shirt does not look right. Adjust the sweatshirt sides with these suggestions, adding trim and fixing the problem.

1. Easy Fix

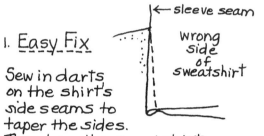

← sleeve seam

wrong side of sweatshirt

Sew in darts on the shirt's side seams to taper the sides. Then hem the sweatshirt.

2. Lacing Fix

Hem the sweatshirt first. Cut a facing for one or both sides of the sweatshirt (4" x 10" long).

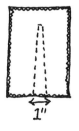

1"

Sew or serge all four edges. Sew an 8" long "V" to attach facing to right side of sweatshirt. Cut open between stitching + flip facing to wrong side of shirt. Add five pairs of buttonholes and lace through a ribbon, shoelace, or cord to draw the sides together.

3. Drawstring Fix

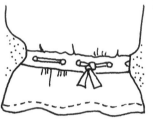

Make a simple casing from Ultrasuede to sew to the waistline or bottom edge of the sweatshirt.

Measure around the shirt and cut Ultrasuede to that length plus ½". The width can be 1", 2"— or a width of your choice.

Cut an <u>even</u> number of holes or slits regularly spaced in the center of the strip.

Sew the strip to the right side of the shirt at the waistline or bottom hem. Then lace through ribbon or cord and pull to draw in the sweatshirt.

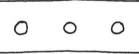

4. Elastic in Casing Fix

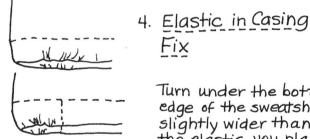

Turn under the bottom edge of the sweatshirt slightly wider than the elastic you plan to insert.

Insert a piece of elastic (sewed in a circle) and sew the casing closed. The bottom edge of the sweatshirt will be gathered to fit close to the body.

Another choice, as illustrated, is to sew in short pieces of elastic only at the sides of the sweatshirt.

5 Applique Additions

✦ THE BASICS ✦ OF SATIN STITCH APPLIQUE

From my experiences in teaching and writing, and from reports from readers and store owners, I know there is always someone new interested in learning how to do traditional machine applique with satin stitching. If you are new to this sewing technique, this section gives you the basics, with tips for successful, professional-looking machine applique. For more detailed instructions, see my books *Sweatshirts with Style* and *Garments with Style*.

Supplies Needed

- paper-backed fusible web for tracing designs
- fabric for applique and for background material
- tear-away stabilizer
- thread to match applique fabric

1 Before any stitching begins, take time to prepare appliques with the correct materials. This way you'll have a better chance at successful stitching. Trace a mirror image of an applique design on the paper side of the fusible web (Fig. 1).

FIGURE 1. Trace a design—a mirror image—on paper-backed fusible web.

2 With the fusible web side against the wrong side of the applique fabric, fuse by pressing and holding the iron on the paper. Follow the fusing instructions that came with the paper-backed fusible web (Fig. 2).

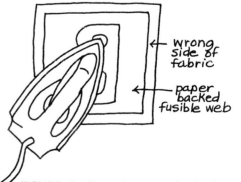

FIGURE 2. Fuse the paper-backed fusible web to the wrong side of the chosen applique fabric.

3 Cut out the applique and remove the paper layer. The applique will now have a smooth fusible backing to apply to the background fabric (Fig. 3).

FIGURE 3. Cut the fused design from the fabric and peel off the paper backing.

4 Fuse the applique shape to the background material. Before sewing, place a piece of stabilizer under the background fabric (Fig. 4) Stabilizer is especially important when applique stitching on knit fabrics like sweatshirt fleece. It prevents wavy looking stitch lines. You want your applique stitches to lie flat and smooth.

FIGURE 4. Press and fuse the applique to fabric. Add stabilizer underneath to prepare for applique stitching.

5 Set the sewing machine for a satin stitch, a stitch width of 2.0, and a short stitch length. Sew around the shape, covering the edge of the applique with the stitching (Fig. 5). You'll learn to pivot and turn the fabrics with the needle down to turn corners and to go around various edges. (You may also prefer a wider applique stitch, such as 2.5 or 3.0.)

FIGURE 5. Sew with a satin stitch, covering the edges of the applique.

➤ **Practice Makes Perfect:** I would not be honest if I didn't admit that this type of sewing will take plenty of practice to achieve a professional look. After all, it differs from garment construction, and it's probably unlike any stitching you've ever done before. Have patience with yourself as you practice, and watch yourself improve with applique stitching as you do more.

6 After stitching is complete, pull the top threads to the wrong side of the fabric, and knot. Remove the stabilizer. Press the fabrics on both sides to smooth them.

After practicing and gaining confidence and skill in your stitching, you'll be ready to work on a sweatshirt. You may want to experiment with other decorative stitches and threads as you become proficient and comfortable with applique.

Be sure to try the following new and unique applique techniques that follow this chapter. You may find them even easier than satin stitch applique.

✦ DIMENSIONAL APPLIQUE ✦ WITH TULLE

Sewing the applique parts to the sweatshirt is quick and easy once you've arranged the flowers in a pleasing way. Give the appliques extra shape by backing them with tulle. This shirt also features Neckline with a Dickey from chapter 2.

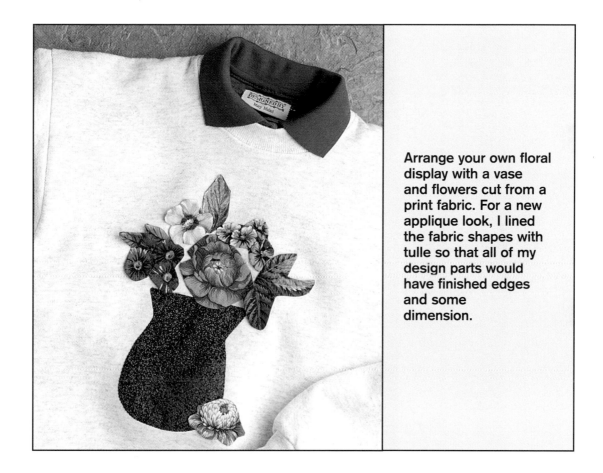

Arrange your own floral display with a vase and flowers cut from a print fabric. For a new applique look, I lined the fabric shapes with tulle so that all of my design parts would have finished edges and some dimension.

Supplies Needed

- ¼ yd. (23cm) solid color fabric
- ¼ yd. (23cm) tulle fabric
- ¼ yd. (23cm) print fabric with medium to large flowers
- small crochet hook
- clear nylon thread

1 Trace the Vase or Flower Pot Applique from page 78 onto a piece of paper and cut it out. Then, trace around the edges onto the right side of the fabric you've chosen. Cut a piece of tulle slightly larger than the container shape (Fig. 1).

right side of fabric

tulle

FIGURE 1. On the right side of the fabric, trace the design. Also cut a piece of tulle slightly larger than the design.

2 Check your stash for flower fabric or purchase new fabric with medium to large size flowers. Cut an assortment of flowers and some

leaves from the fabric, leaving an extra edge of fabric all the way around (Fig. 2).

cutting lines

FIGURE 2. Use flower and leaf designs from printed fabrics, making sure to cut extra fabric around each design.

I found it easiest to plan my bouquet by cutting out a variety of flowers, flower groupings, and leaves. Then cut a piece of tulle to place on top of each flower and leaf. Pin the tulle to the right side of the fabric for both the flower container and the flowers (Fig. 3).

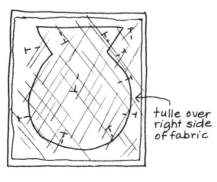

tulle over right side of fabric

FIGURE 3. Place the tulle over the design, and pin it in place.

3 At the sewing machine, shorten the stitch length to 2.0. Sew around the edges of the flower container, the flowers, and the leaves. You'll have clearly drawn edges to follow on the container, but you will have to guess or round out the stitching on the flower edges because many flowers and leaves have jagged or irregular edges. After stitching, trim and clip the seam allowances to approximately ⅛" (3mm). Work on the fabric side, clipping to inside corners and trimming back fabrics from points (Fig. 4).

wrong side of fabric

FIGURE 4. Clip and trim the corners of the seam allowances.

4 Press the fabric pieces from the fabric side. Carefully cut a slash in the center of the tulle layer only and draw the fabric out through the opening (Fig. 5). Finger press the fabric edges and use a small crochet hook inserted in the slash to slide beneath the seam allowances to gently prod and poke the fabric edges out (Fig. 6). The crochet hook with its rounded end works better than scissors or sharp points for pushing the seam edge out.

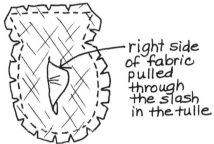

FIGURE 5. Cut a slash in the tulle layer and pull the right side of the fabric out through the opening.

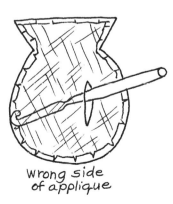

FIGURE 6. Slide a crochet hook through the slash in the tulle to push out the seam allowances and fabric edges.

5 Press each piece of the design from the back and front. Then lay out and plan your own floral bouquet on the sweatshirt.

6 Pin each piece in place with at least two pins. On larger pieces, such as the flower container, use many pins. Use clear nylon thread to sew each piece to the shirt. This way the thread will blend with each fabric color and produce an invisible attachment.

7 Sew the flower container first. I used a small blanket stitch so the stitching just catches the edge of the fabric (Fig. 7). Next, sew on the flowers and leaves. Some may overlap the edge of the container. Use the same blanket stitch to sew around the shapes or straightstitch inside the shapes, making veins in the leaves, for example, to secure the pieces to the shirt (Fig. 8). This way, the applique shapes have more dimension when the edges are not sewn down. I did not use a stabilizer under the sweatshirt while I sewed, but you may prefer to add some if the stitching puckers too much.

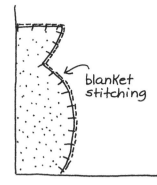

FIGURE 7. With clear thread and a narrow blanket stitch, you'll hardly be able to see how the vase is attached to the sweatshirt.

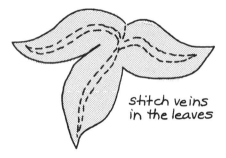

FIGURE 8. Attach flowers or leaves to the shirt by straightstitching veins or petal sections instead of sewing around the edges.

The dimensional applique with tulle is a quick-and-easy applique method that I was inspired to try by an article in the September 1995 issue of *Threads* magazine. (See the Resources list on page 147.)

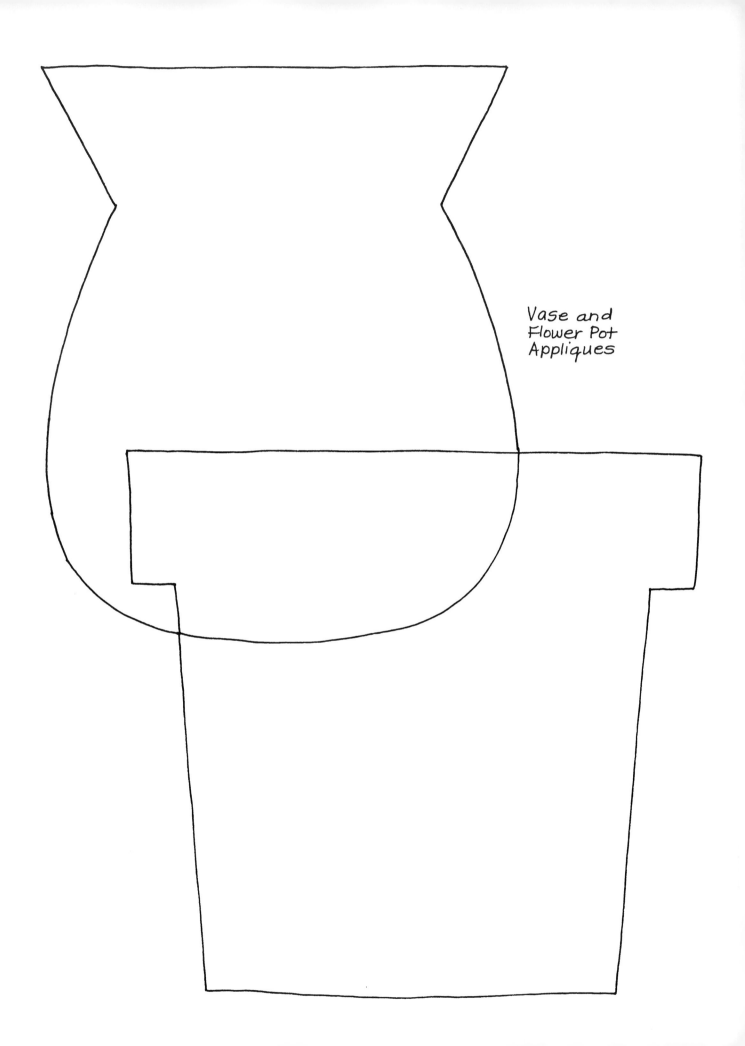

Vase and
Flower Pot
Appliques

✦ SCRUB STITCH APPLIQUE ✦

Your choice of fabric and design can lead to a variety of looks for this whimsical and oh-so-easy applique stitch.

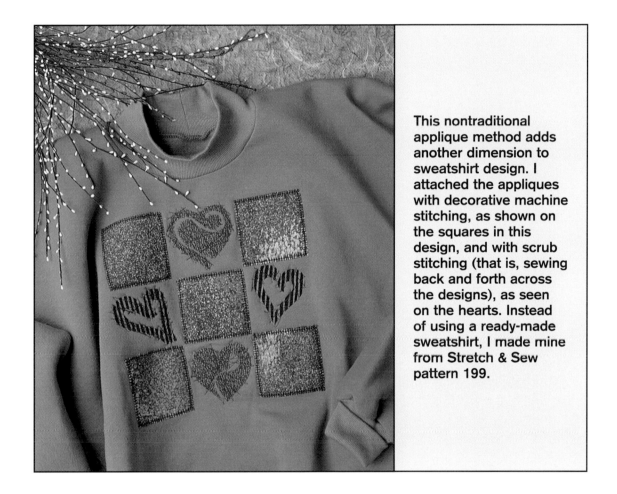

This nontraditional applique method adds another dimension to sweatshirt design. I attached the appliques with decorative machine stitching, as shown on the squares in this design, and with scrub stitching (that is, sewing back and forth across the designs), as seen on the hearts. Instead of using a ready-made sweatshirt, I made mine from Stretch & Sew pattern 199.

Supplies Needed

- ¼ yd. (23cm) paper-backed fusible web
- ¼ yd. (23cm) fabric for applique
- ¼ yd. (23cm) water-soluble or rinse-away stabilizer

1 The shirt in the photograph features 3″ (7.5cm) squares in a nine-patch formation with four different heart designs between. The squares are fused and sewn with a decorative machine stitch. Trace the four heart designs from the book (Fig. 1) onto paper-backed fusible web, fuse them to the wrong side of the applique fabrics, and cut out the shapes. Fuse the fabric hearts to the spaces in the design. Now you're almost ready to begin stitching.

FIGURE 1. Four heart designs for scrub applique stitching.

2 On the back of the sweatshirt or other background fabric, place and pin a piece of water-soluble or rinse-away stabilizer. When so much stitching is added to the shirt, it's easiest to wet the stabilizer to remove it rather than to try to tear it away between all the stitching lines.

3 With a straightstitch setting on the machine, start sewing across the applique design. When you reach the other side, stop stitching, pivot the fabric and sew across in a different direction either by turning the fabric or using the reverse sewing button (Fig. 2). You can sew past the fabric edges, as I did, or stop just over the edges (Fig. 3). Obviously, you won't be covering all the

edges with stitches, but the design is fused in place and all the straightstitching definitely secures it to the background. Stitch back and forth until you feel you have enough stitches and stop.

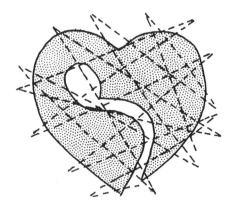

FIGURE 2. Use the straightstitch with a scrubbing motion, sewing straight across, back and forth, and over the edges.

FIGURE 3. Straightstitch just to the fabric edges.

See how easy it is? Now you can experiment with different thread colors or perhaps even different machine stitches, such as the zigzag stitch.

✦ SCISSOR CUTTINGS APPLIQUE ✦

Scherenschnitte, the German word for "scissor cuttings," can be used for this intricate applique cutting. This may remind you of paper-cutting exercises in elementary school, because it is cutting that requires patience and a little time. But it's worth it to get the detailed cut shape to trim a sweatshirt.

Cut a stylish applique from a single piece of fabric to trim a sweatshirt. I chose a velour-like knit fabric that will not fray. After cutting the design, I fused it to the shirt and sewed around the edge with clear thread and a narrow blanket stitch to conceal the stitching line. To further enhance the sweatshirt, I added a Funnel Drawstring Collar using the instructions on page 27.

Supplies Needed

- 9" (23cm) square non-fray fabric, such as a knit, knit velour, felt, Ultrasuede
- 9" (23cm) square paper-backed fusible web

- small embroidery scissors or other small scissors with sharp blades
- 10" (25.5cm) square of tear-away stabilizer
- clear nylon thread

1 Trace the Scissor Cuttings Applique from page 83 on the back of paper-backed fusible web. Fuse the tracing to the wrong side of the non-fray fabric, making sure the paper fuses completely to the fabric.

2 Begin cutting the design in the center. Instead of poking the tips of the scissors through the paper and fabric on the line of a design shape you plan to cut out, poke the tips through the center area and then cut to the edges, continuing to cut around to remove the shape (Fig. 1).

FIGURE 1. Begin cutting in the center of design areas.

3 If the paper-backed fusible web loosens or shifts as you cut, take time to re-fuse it to the fabric. The lines of the design need to stay in place for accurate cutting. Try to handle the fabric and paper backing as carefully as you can as you cut.

4 The last cutting will be the outside edge of the design. Cut from the edge of the fabric to the lines of the design's shape (Fig. 2).

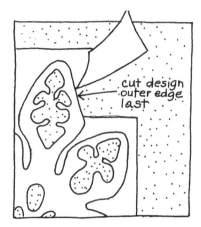

cut design outer edge last

FIGURE 2. Cut the outside edge of the design.

5 Remove the paper backing and position the design on the sweatshirt. Though the design appears square in the book, I positioned it as a diamond shape on the shirt (Fig. 3).

FIGURE 3. Place the scissor cuttings design in a diamond position on a shirt front or back.

6 Place and pin the stabilizer under the sweatshirt and then sew around the center circle of the design and then the outer edge. A straight stitch works well, as does a narrow zigzag. Clear nylon thread or thread to match the applique fabric is a good suggestion for an invisible or hidden stitch attachment. Instead of seeing the stitching, the eye sees the beautiful, intricate applique design. Add more stitching if you want the design to be more secure.

Experiment with designs you cut yourself. All those paper snowflakes you cut as a child might help you as you try new scissor-cutting appliques.

scissor cuttings
applique

6 *Other Decorating Ideas*

✦ LARGE-COLLAR MOCK FRONT ✦

You might not guess that this large collar is really two polo collars. My favorite way to attach the ribbon and button is with safety pins, so it's easy to remove before laundering or to replace it with different trim.

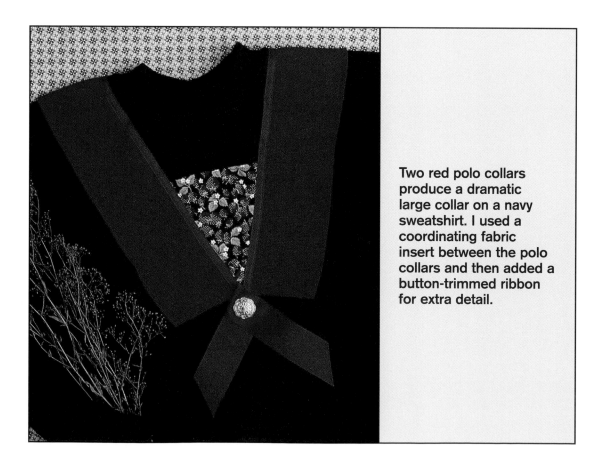

Two red polo collars produce a dramatic large collar on a navy sweatshirt. I used a coordinating fabric insert between the polo collars and then added a button-trimmed ribbon for extra detail.

Supplies Needed

- one sweatshirt with set-in sleeves
- two matching polo/finished-edge knit collars
- 9" (23cm) square of fabric for fabric insert
- 2 yds. (183cm) of ¼" (6mm) ribbon or braid to cover collar edges
- ¼ yd. (23cm) paper-backed fusible web
- ¼ yd. (23cm) stabilizer (optional)
- 12" (30.5cm) of 1½" (4cm) ribbon for tie trim
- one button (optional)

1 Find and mark the sweatshirt's center front, using the instructions on page 5. Draw the line at least 12" (30.5cm) down from the neckline edge.

2 Examine your collars before pinning them to the sweatshirt. Some collars have a thick or raveling edge and this should be trimmed off so the edges are flat. Place one end of each collar along the shoulder seams on each side of the neck opening. Leave about 1" (2.5cm) free on each side of the ribbing, or more if you plan to use a wide ribbon or braid to cover the collar edges (Fig. 1).

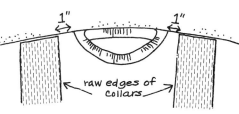

FIGURE 1. Place one end of each collar 1" from the neck ribbing on each side of the neckline.

3 Position the other ends of the collars along the center front line and pin in place (Fig. 2). If the collars are long and meet too low on the shirt, open the shoulder seams of the shirt, just enough to insert the upper ends of the collars (Fig. 3). Adjust the collar length on the shirt front until you like the place where the lower collar ends meet on the shirt center front.

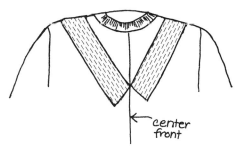

FIGURE 2. Bring the other ends of the collars together at center front.

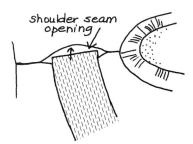

FIGURE 3. Open the sweatshirt shoulder seams to insert the collar ends if the collars need to be shortened for correct placement on the shirt front.

4 With thread to match the collars, topstitch the upper collar edges to the shoulder seams (or seam allowances, if you inserted the collar ends) of the sweatshirt (Fig. 4). After stitching, cut away the excess collar lengths if you inserted the collar ends into the seam allowances.

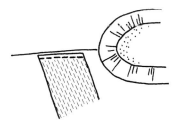

FIGURE 4. Use matching thread to sew the collar ends to the shoulder area.

5 Slide a piece of paper under the collars at the center front to determine the size and location of the fabric insert (Fig. 5). Draw lines on the paper along the inside collar edges. Remove the paper and add ½" (1.3cm) to each side of the insert lines and cut out the insert pattern (Fig. 6). Place the pattern on a folded piece of fabric and cut (Fig. 7). Slide the fabric insert under the collars and pin in place, making sure that the collar sides will cover the side edges of the fabric insert. The insert top edge can be stitched down or left unstitched because the next sewing will secure the insert and the collars to the shirt.

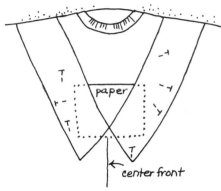

FIGURE 5. Insert paper between the collars and trace the raw edges of the collars on the paper.

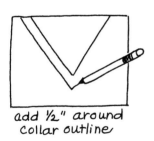

add ½" around collar outline

FIGURE 6. To make the insert pattern, add ½" to both sides of the collar outline.

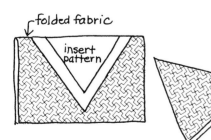

FIGURE 7. Cut the insert pattern from a piece of folded fabric.

6 Using a generous number of pins, pin the two collars to the shirt. Then, sew the long inside edges to the shirt, using a straight or narrow zigzag stitch and sewing close to the edges (Fig. 8).

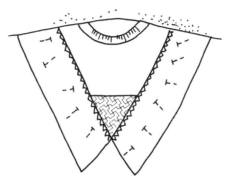

FIGURE 8. Sew the raw edges of the collar to the shirt. Use plenty of pins to hold the collars in place.

7 Cut a piece of ribbon or braid to cover each collar edge. Fuse strips of paper-backed fusible web to the wrong sides of the ribbon strips. Remove the paper backing and fuse the ribbon strips over the raw edges of the collars, remembering to turn under the ends at both the shoulder edge and the center of the shirt. Sew the ribbons to the shirt (Fig. 9). I did not use stabilizer under the sweatshirt for this sewing, but if you notice any stitching problems or puckering, stop sewing and add stabilizer to the wrong side of the sweatshirt.

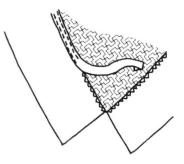

FIGURE 9. Cover the inner edges of the collars by stitching ribbon over the edges.

8 To make the ribbon tie below the collars, taper the ends of the 12" (30.5cm) ribbon. Fold the ribbon in half and bring the fold to meet the side of the ribbon (Fig. 10). Center the button on the folded ribbon and sew or pin the ribbon and button to the sweatshirt. I like the choice of removing them for laundry or for a change of colors.

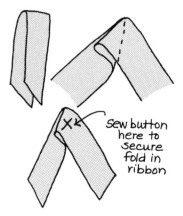

Sew button here to secure fold in ribbon

FIGURE 10. Fold a 12" ribbon in half and then bring the fold to the side of the ribbon to form a tie to trim the sweatshirt.

Another option for this mock front trim is to use a knit collar as a pattern and make your own collars from other kinds of fabric.

✦ MOCK FRONT CARDIGAN ✦ WITH DICKEY INSERT

Add a pre-made knit dickey to a sweatshirt neckline to give this shirt a layered look. With all of the subtle changes that I made to the shirt, it no longer resembles a sweatshirt.

This sweatshirt only looks like it opens in front. I created the illusion by sewing a dickey to the shirt neckline and using braid trim to outline the edges of the faux opening.

Supplies Needed

- one sweatshirt with set-in sleeves
- one knit dickey
- 2 yds. (183cm) of decorative braid
- ¼ yd. (23cm) stabilizer (optional)
- 16″ (40.5cm) ribbon for front tie
- 1 yd. (91.5cm) tricot knit fusible interfacing (optional)
- ¼ yd. (23cm) paper-backed fusible web (optional)

1 Try on the dickey to make sure it fits over your head. Then examine its fabric. One of the dickeys I used seemed thin, so I fused tricot knit interfacing to the wrong sides of the front and back of the dickey.

2 Using a chalk marker or washable marking pen, mark the center front line of the sweatshirt from the top of the neck to the top of the ribbing at the shirt bottom, following the instructions on page 5.

3 Fit the dickey inside the sweatshirt neckline. The easiest way to do this is on a dressmaker's form or on yourself. Line up and pin together the shoulder seams of the dickey and the sweatshirt. Use many pins to hold the dickey and the sweatshirt together on both the front and back (Fig. 1).

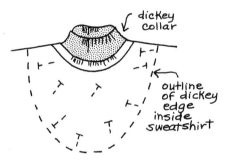

FIGURE 1. Place the dickey inside the sweatshirt and pin the two together.

4 Lay the sweatshirt and dickey on a flat surface with the front facing up. Using a chalk marker or a washable marking pen mark 1″ (2.5cm) on each side of the sweatshirt neck ribbing. Determine where the bottom edge of the dickey lies inside the shirt and on the shirt front line, mark a point 1″ (2.5cm) above the end of the dickey (Fig. 2).

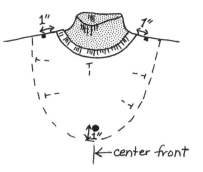

FIGURE 2. Mark 1″ on each side of the neck ribbing and 1″ above the bottom front edge of the dickey.

5 Draw a straight line from the shoulder marks to the center front mark, creating a V in the shirt front (Fig. 3). On the shirt back, mark 1″ (2.5cm) below the neck ribbing and draw a line between the shoulder seams (Fig. 4).

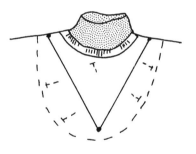

FIGURE 3. With a washable marker, draw lines to connect the shoulder and center front marks.

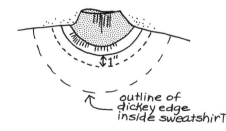

FIGURE 4. Draw a line 1″ below the neck ribbing around the back of the sweatshirt.

6 Staystitch on the front V lines and continue around the back of the shirt neck, sewing along the line 1″ (2.5cm) below the ribbing. This stitching will attach the dickey to the sweatshirt (Fig. 5).

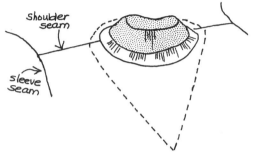

FIGURE 5. Sew around the sweatshirt back and front on the lines drawn on the shirt.

7 Carefully cut the sweatshirt away inside the stitching lines, leaving a narrow ⅛″ (3mm) seam allowance along the front V. At the shoulder seams, cut the fleece right below the ribbing, leaving extra fleece fabric above the stitching line (Fig. 6). Turn under and pin the extra fabric on the back of the shirt. Sew down the folded edge of the fabric. Now there will be two rows of stitching on the sweatshirt back neckline (Fig. 7).

FIGURE 6. Cut away the back neck ribbing, leaving extra fabric above the stitching line.

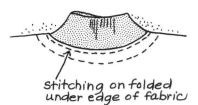

FIGURE 7. Finish the back neckline by turning under and stitching the sweatshirt fabric at the neck edge.

8 Next, cover the raw edges of the sweatshirt fleece on the front of the shirt to create the mock V-neck cardigan. Measure and cut a piece of braid to cover the right side of the V-neck. Pin or fuse (with strips of paper-backed fusible web) the braid to the right side of the shirt, covering the raw edge of the sweatshirt fabric and turning under the braid end at the shoulder (Fig. 8). Sew on both sides of the braid. If you notice any puckering or difficulty with the fabric while sewing, add a piece of stabilizer to the wrong side of the sweatshirt.

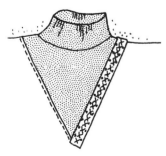

FIGURE 8. Fuse or pin decorative braid on the right side of the V on the shirt front.

9 Determine the length of the braid on the left side of the V. Place the remaining braid at the opposite shoulder seam, down the left side of the V, and to a point 6″ (15cm) beyond the end of the V. Then fold a tuck in the braid so it can be directed to the bottom edge of the shirt, ending at the center front (Fig. 9), allowing an extra 1″ (2.5cm) of braid.

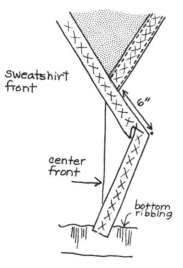

FIGURE 9. Lay the braid on the left side of the V neck edge, straight to a point 6″ from the end of the V and then direct it to the sweatshirt bottom edge on the center front line.

10 Fuse strips of paper-backed fusible web to the back of the braid and then fuse the braid to the shirt. Start at the shoulder seam where the end of the braid will be turned under to cover the end of the back neckline stitching and continue down the front, to the 6″ (15cm) mark. Before fusing farther, cut the 16″ (40.5cm) ribbon in half and insert the end of one piece under the braid

(Fig. 10). Then, continue fusing the braid to the sweatshirt, turn under the end at the top edge of the bottom ribbing, and trim off any extra braid at this point. Sew the braid to the sweatshirt.

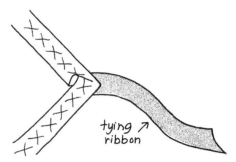

FIGURE 10. Insert an 8″ piece of ribbon under the tuck in the braid.

11 Sew the second piece of ribbon approximately 2″ (5cm) from the other ribbon (Fig. 11). Tie the ribbons together. Another option is to add buttons for a double-breasted cardigan appearance.

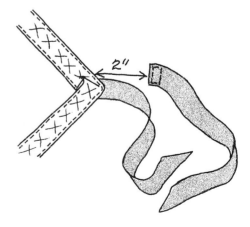

FIGURE 11. Pin and sew the second piece of ribbon 2″ from the first piece.

✦ MOCK FRONT PLACKET ✦ WITH TOGGLE CLOSURES

Sometimes interesting closures can provide the inspiration for a new sweatshirt idea. Here the toggles are decorative rather than functional.

I overlapped wide fabric strips on this sweatshirt to create the look of a placket. Although the placket doesn't open, the toggle closures make it look realistic. I also enhanced the neckline by adding an overlapping funnel collar from chapter 2, but I eliminated the buttons and buttonholes.

Supplies Needed

- one sweatshirt
- ½ yd. (46cm) fabric for placket
- two toggle buttons or purchased toggle closures
- 1 yd. (91.5cm) cord for making closures
- Small pieces of Ultrasuede, vinyl, or other stable non-fray fabric for making closures

1 Staystitch close to the sweatshirt neck ribbing, following the directions on page 6. Cut away the ribbing and excess fabric above the staystitching line. Press the neckline to flatten the edges.

Using a chalk marker or a wash-able marking pen, mark the center front line on the shirt, as instructed on page 5.

2 Cut two pieces of fabric 8″ x 11″ (20.5 x 28cm). Fold the fabrics in half with right sides together. Sew them together lengthwise ¼″ (6mm) from the edge (Fig. 1). Turn the two pieces right side out and press so the seamline is on the center of the back (Fig. 2).

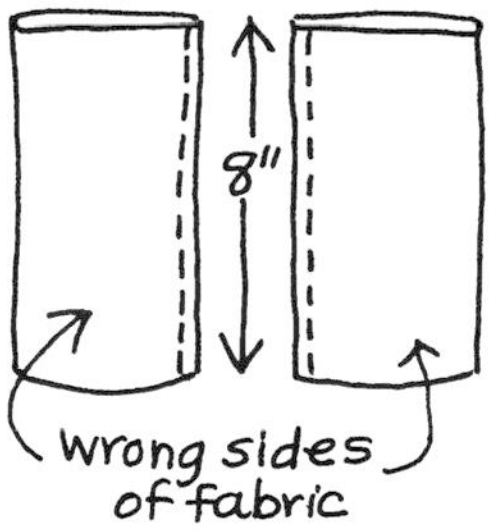

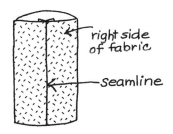

FIGURE 1. Fold the two fabrics with right sides together and meet the 8″ edges. Sew ¼″ from the raw edges.

FIGURE 2. Place the seamline in the center of the back of each fabric piece.

3 With the right sides of the fabric pieces facing up, place the left piece ¾″ (2cm) over the right piece to overlap the two. Topstitch ½″ (1.3cm) from the folded edge of the top piece to hold the two fabric pieces together (Fig. 3).

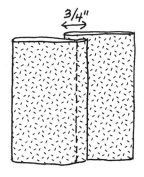

FIGURE 3. Overlap the two pieces ¾″ and topstitch ½″ from the edge of the top fabric piece, to hold the two pieces together.

4 Turn under ½″ (1.3cm) of the cut edge at the bottom of the fabric piece and press (Fig. 4). The piece is now ready to be pinned and sewn to the shirt.

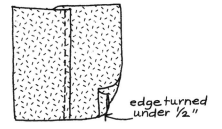

FIGURE 4. Turn under and press the bottom edge of the placket piece to prepare to attach it to the shirt.

5 Position and pin the fabric front to the center front of the sweatshirt. Make sure that the top edges completely cover the rounded sweatshirt neckline (Fig. 5). Use lots of pins on the edges and center of the fabric. Sew around the edges. You may want to reinforce the sewing across the bottom edge to make it look like an actual placket (Fig. 6).

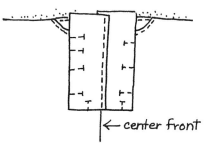

FIGURE 5. Center and pin the placket on the sweatshirt front, making sure the top edges cover the curve of the neckline.

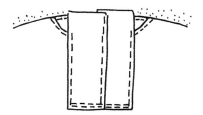

FIGURE 6. Sew the sides and bottom edges of the placket to the sweatshirt.

Turn to the wrong side of the shirt neckline and stitch on the fleece edge and through the added fabric. Cut away the excess fabric above the stitching line (Fig. 7).

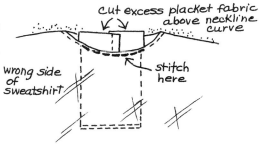

FIGURE 7. On the wrong side of the sweatshirt, sew the placket to the neckline curve and cut off the extra fabric extending above the neckline.

6 Purchased toggle closures come ready to sew on, but if you want to customize the look with your own colors, it's easy to make your own. Toggle buttons have two large holes through which you can insert cord. Cut four pieces of cord 6″ (15cm) long. Loop through each button and sew across the cords 1″ (2.5cm) from the button (Fig. 8). Fold the other two cords in half to form the loops. Sew across the cords as you did for the button sides 1¼″ (3cm) from the end of the loop (Fig. 9).

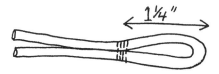

FIGURE 9. Fold the remaining 6″ cords in half and sew across to form a 1¼″ loop.

7 Trace the Toggle End Pattern from the book (Fig. 10) onto a piece of paper and cut it out. Use it to cut four end pieces from Ultrasuede, vinyl, or other non-fray fabric.

Place the ends of the cords under the end fabric pieces, pin the cords and ends to the shirt, and sew to secure (Fig. 11). I recommend that you sew twice across the side that covers the cord ends.

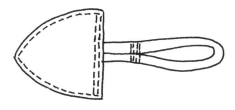

FIGURE 11. Sew the toggle end shape over the cord ends.

Now that the mock placket and toggles are complete, it's time to select a new collar or neckline alteration. I chose to add an overlapping funnel collar without buttons or buttonholes.

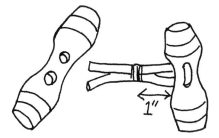

FIGURE 8. Loop 6″ cords through two toggle buttons.

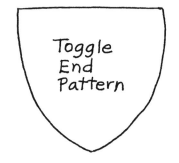

Toggle End Pattern

FIGURE 10. Toggle end pattern.

✦ NORDIC SWEATSHIRT ✦

Adding a front yoke to a sweatshirt can result in a variety of styles and effects, depending on the fabric used. Well-chosen trim will enhance the overall effect.

Add Scandinavian style to a sweatshirt with a front yoke, braid trim, and Lycra binding around the neckline and front opening. This is no ordinary sweatshirt! I've added a pair of hand knit mittens from my collection and a silver ski pin to complement the Nordic theme of the sweatshirt.

Supplies Needed

- one sheet of tissue paper for pattern making
- ½ yd. (46cm) paper-backed fusible web
- one sweatshirt with set-in sleeves
- ½ yd. (46cm) fabric for bib front
- ⅛ yd. (11.5cm) Lycra fabric for neck binding
- 1½ yds. (137cm) each of several decorative braids
- buttons or pewter clasps (see Resources on page 147)

1 The first addition to the Nordic sweatshirt is the fabric front bib or panel. To make a pattern for this panel, lay a piece of tissue paper over the shirt front. Trace the curved neckline and shoulders, and extend straight lines from the ends of the shoulders. As a guide for the bottom edge of the panel, measure down 8" (20.5cm) from the ribbing center front. Draw a line across to connect the side lines (Fig. 1).

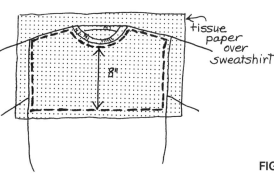

FIGURE 1. Trace the outline of the front panel on a piece of white tissue paper placed over the sweatshirt front.

2 Trace the panel outline on paper-backed fusible web. Fuse to the wrong side of the panel fabric and cut out the shape. Place the fused fabric panel on the sweatshirt front and fuse in place. Use a narrow zigzag stitch along the edges of the fabric (Fig. 2).

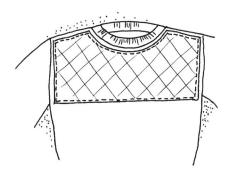

FIGURE 2. Fuse and baste the panel to the sweatshirt front.

3 Using a chalk marker or washable marking pen, mark a 6" (15cm) center front line from the top of the neck edge of the shirt, using the instructions on page 5. Sew ⅛" (3mm) on both sides of the line, with one stitch across the bottom. Cut in a straight line between the stitching lines (Fig. 3).

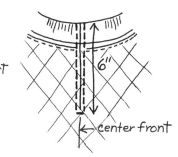

FIGURE 3. To create an opening in the shirt front, sew on each side of a 6" line down center front. Cut between the stitching lines.

4 Measure the neck edge and the opening in the shirt front to determine the length of binding you'll need, using the instructions on page 6. Cut a 1-½" (4cm) wide strip of Lycra fabric to the measured length. Beginning at the back neck, pin the binding strip, right side of binding to right side of shirt, around the entire shirt neck and opening (Fig. 4).

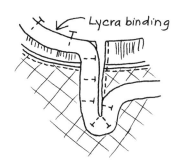

FIGURE 4. Pin a strip of Lycra fabric around the neckline and on the front neckline opening.

Do not stretch either the Lycra or the neck ribbing. Sew on the binding with a ¼" (6mm) seam allowance. At the bottom of the front opening, turn the sweatshirt and binding so you can sew straight across (Fig. 5).

Overlap and sew the ends of the binding when it meets at the back of the neck (Fig. 6).

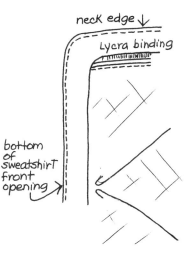

FIGURE 5. Open the front opening of the sweatshirt so it is in a straight line when you sew the binding to the shirt.

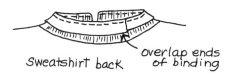

FIGURE 6. On the back neckline, to one side of center back, overlap the ends of the Lycra fabric binding.

5 Trim away the corners of ribbing where the binding curves from the neck edge to the front opening (Fig. 7).

FIGURE 7. Cut away the corners of ribbing at the neckline edges.

6 Turn the loose edge of the binding to the inside of the shirt, pin it into place over the previous stitching line, and sew from the right side of the shirt, sewing in the "ditch" between the binding and the shirt (Fig. 8). If there is excess binding fabric on the back, you may want to trim it away. Because Lycra is a non-fray fabric, there's no need to worry about raveling.

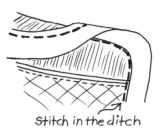

FIGURE 8. Sew the second edge of the binding to the neckline by stitching in the ditch from the right side of the shirt's neckline.

7 Sew extra trim to the fabric panel, if you wish. The shirt illustrated features a strip of braiding on the front panel (Fig. 9).

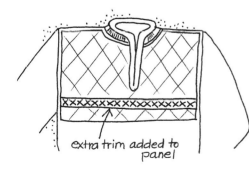

FIGURE 9. A piece of decorative braid is added to trim the front panel.

8 Next, sew braid trim around the edges of the front panel and around the neck opening. I chose a narrow braid, which is easier to pin and sew around the neckline curve. Fold in tucks on the braid to work it around the front opening (Fig. 10). Unless the braid you selected is very narrow, sew on both edges to attach the braid to the shirt.

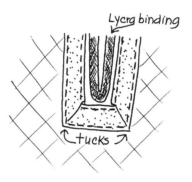

FIGURE 10. Fold tucks into the decorative braid to work it around the shirt front opening.

9 No closures are required for the shirt neckline, but I like to use the pewter ones to give an authentic Norwegian sweater appearance to the sweatshirt. (See Resources for a mail-order source for these unique clasps.)

Another option is to sew one button on each side of the opening, sew a narrow piece of elastic beneath one button, and loop the elastic over the opposite button (Fig. 11).

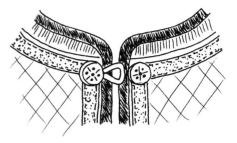

FIGURE 11. Two buttons with an elastic loop make an attractive closure with a Nordic look.

10 While trimming the sleeves is also optional, it adds so much to the Nordic look. The easiest way to work on the sleeves is to open the seam about 8" (20.5cm) up from the cuff. Mark a line 1" (2.5cm) above the cuff ribbing and place the bottom edge of a piece of braid along the line (Fig. 12). Fuse or pin the braids in place before sewing them to the sleeve. Afterward, sew or serge the sleeve seams closed again.

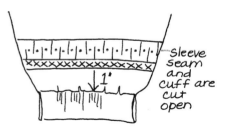

FIGURE 12. Open the cuffs and sleeve seams to sew decorative braid to the sleeves.

The 1994 Winter Olympics in Lillehammer, Norway, inspired me to create this sweatshirt. It's perfect for women, men, and children.

✦ Easy-Lace Buttonhole Trim ✦

This classy addition is fun and quick to sew, and it's easy to change the lacing.

For this clever sweat-shirt, I used Ultrasuede squares to encircle the neckline. I cut button holes as straight lines inside the stitched areas on the squares. After stitching and cutting, I laced a silk scarf that I salvaged from my accessory collection from 10 years ago (some things are hard to throw away or sell at a rummage sale!) through the openings around the neckline.

Supplies Needed

- ¼ yd. (23cm) paper-backed fusible web (optional)
- small pieces of Ultrasuede (or other fabric) or 2″ (5cm) wide strip
- one sweatshirt
- 40″ (102cm) or longer tie, ribbon, or scarf for lacing through holes

1 Trace the Buttonhole Square Template from the book (Fig. 1) onto a piece of paper and cut it out. On the paper pattern, cut out the narrow rectangles inside the template. These will be the buttonhole outlines (Fig. 2).

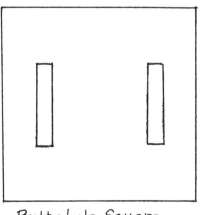

Buttonhole Square template

FIGURE 1. Buttonhole square template.

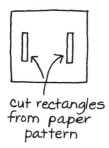

cut rectangles
from paper
pattern

FIGURE 2. With a sharp pair of scissors, cut out the two narrow rectangles from inside the paper pattern of the buttonhole square.

2 The squares can be fused to the sweatshirt or pinned in place. If you decide to fuse the squares on before sewing, trace five squares on paper-backed fusible web. (Trace and use more than five squares if you want the squares closer together around the neckline.) Fuse the patterns to the wrong side of Ultrasuede and cut out the squares. If you plan to pin on the squares instead of fusing, draw the five outlines directly on the back of the Ultrasuede and cut them from the fabric (Fig. 3). Do not cut out the buttonhole rectangles as they are a stitching guide only.

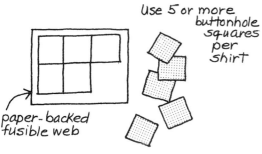

Use 5 or more
buttonhole
squares
per
shirt

paper-backed
fusible web

FIGURE 3. Cut five buttonhole squares from fabric. You can fuse or pin them to the sweatshirt.

3 Fuse with a press cloth over the Ultrasuede or pin the squares around the neckline. I placed mine ½″ (1.3cm) below the ribbing or sweatshirt neckline. One is at the center back, two are on the raglan seams on the shirt back, and two more are on the front raglan seams (Fig. 4).

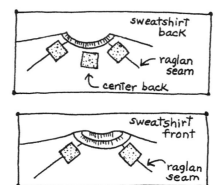

sweatshirt
back

raglan
seam

center back

sweatshirt
front

raglan
seam

FIGURE 4. Place the five buttonholes around the sweatshirt neckline on the four raglan seams and also the center back.

With a chalk marker or washable marking pen, draw the buttonhole outlines on the right side of each square (Fig. 5). As you sew and handle the squares, you may need to redraw the lines, so keep the pen and pattern handy.

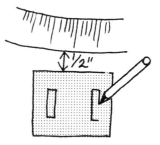

FIGURE 5. On each square, place the paper pattern over the top and trace the rectangular openings with a washable marking pen.

4 Sew the squares to the shirt, stitching close to the edge of the fabric. Ultrasuede is a great choice of fabric because it won't fray and the edges are stable; plus it looks so classy. Then sew around each buttonhole outline, using a short stitch length (Fig. 6).

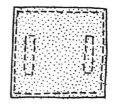

FIGURE 6. Sew the edges of the squares and also sew around the buttonhole outlines.

5 Cut a slit opening inside each buttonhole outline, using a buttonhole cutter or a sharp pair of scissors (Fig. 7).

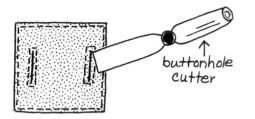

FIGURE 7. Cut each buttonhole open with a straight line but between the stitching lines.

6 The buttonholes are ready for lacing (Fig. 8). Make your own 40" (102cm) tie, rummage in your scarf collection, or select ribbon for the sweatshirt. If you make the lacing squares in a color to match the sweatshirt, you'll have lots of options for scarf/tie colors.

FIGURE 8. Lace a narrow scarf, ribbon, or tie through the buttonholes encircling your sweatshirt neckline.

Here's another lacing idea for someone who likes to sew buttonholes on the machine: Sew pairs of buttonholes around the neckline instead of using the fabric squares. Make sure to fuse lightweight interfacing to the back of the shirt where the buttonholes will be located and then also use a stabilizer under the fabric while sewing the buttonholes.

✦ FLEECE-WOVEN FRONT ✦

Take advantage of the non-fray edges of sweatshirt fleece and weave extra strips right into the shirt. If you're nervous about this project, try working on scrap fabrics first.

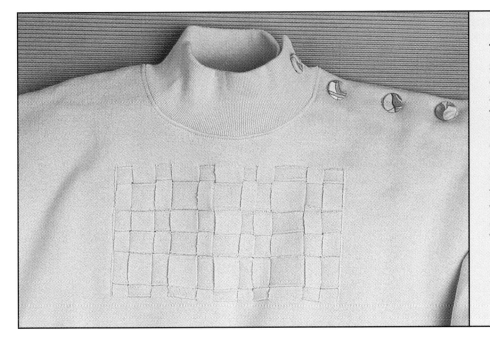

The weaving on this shirt is created by cutting the shirt front and inserting strips of fleece. The idea scared me at first, but after I experimented on a spare piece of sweatshirt fabric and found that it worked, I felt confident enough to cut a sweatshirt front. The neckline of this shirt is the Funnel Collar with Buttons and Shoulder Opening from chapter 2.

Supplies Needed

- small pieces of sweatshirt fleece for experimenting
- leftover fabric from the same sweatshirt (cut from the sleeve or hemline) or other fleece
- rotary mat to fit inside sweatshirt
- rotary cutter
- one sweatshirt with set-in sleeves
- ¼ yd. (23cm) fusible tricot knit interfacing

- ¼ yd. (23cm) tear-away stabilizer
- small pieces of Stitch Witchery or other fusible web

1 Find sweatshirt fabric to cut in strips for the crosswise strips in the weaving. (Weavers call these weft strips.) The fabric can be a different color or colors from the sweatshirt or fabric cut from another part of the sweatshirt such as the sleeves or hem. I used

fabric from the sleeve ends, which I removed to make two-piece cuffs on the sweatshirt (Fig. 1).

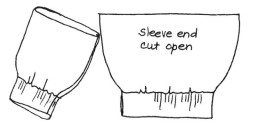

FIGURE 1. Sleeve ends cut from the sweatshirt can be used for fleece weaving on the sweatshirt front. Cut both sleeve ends open on the seam line.

2 Measure the extra fleece to determine the width of the woven section in the shirt. My fabric was 7" x 10" (18 x 25.5cm) wide so I planned my woven section to be 5" x 9" (12.5 x 23cm). If you have enough fabric, compare the look of strips cut with the fabric grain and strips cut across the grain (Fig. 2). If you are using fabric cut from the same shirt, you'll often have no choice but to use the fabric across the grain, as I did. Cut the loose fabric strips for weaving on a rotary mat with a rotary cutter. Cut each strip the same width or cut them of various widths, as I chose to do.

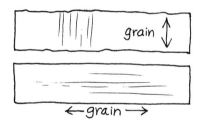

FIGURE 2. Compare the edges and appearance of fleece strips cut across and with the grain. You may have a preference.

3 Make a paper pattern of the outline of your weaving area. Try on the shirt and pin the outline in the location where you want the weaving to be positioned. Trace the outline onto the sweatshirt front with a chalk marker or washable marking pen (Fig. 3).

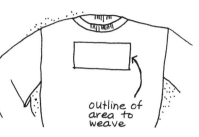

FIGURE 3. Position and trace the weaving area outline on the sweatshirt.

4 This is the step where you'll be cutting the sweatshirt. But before you do that, the most important thing to do is to slide the rotary cutting mat inside the sweatshirt and beneath the outline area (Fig. 4).

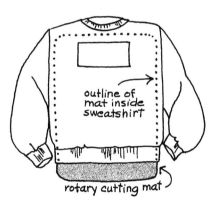

FIGURE 4. Don't forget to slide a rotary cutting mat inside the sweatshirt before cutting the shirt!

Draw straight vertical lines on the shirt inside the weaving outline as a guide for cutting or simply cut with a steady hand (Fig. 5). Count the two side lines of the outline as two cutting lines and add more between them, making sure you cut an *even* number of lines

(Fig. 6). Again, you can vary the width of each strip you cut so some of the vertical strips will be wider than others. Start and stop cutting at the top and bottom lines of the frame. You will be cutting only *vertical* lines in the sweatshirt.

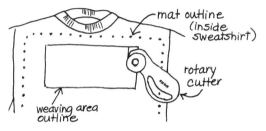

FIGURE 5. Cut an even number of vertical lines in the weaving area on the shirt.

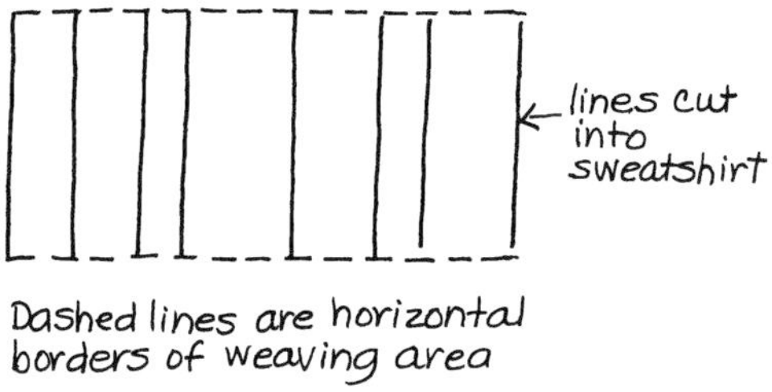

FIGURE 6. Vary the widths of the strips cut into the shirt or cut them all the same width.

5 Now you're ready to weave through the extra fabric strips you cut earlier. Leave extra fabric extended on each side of the design area, with all ends inside the shirt. Pin the ends of the strips to the sides of the weaving outline to hold the weaving together (Fig. 7).

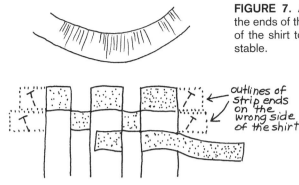

FIGURE 7. As you weave, pin the ends of the strips to the back of the shirt to keep the weaving stable.

➤**Catching the Loose Weaving:** If you want to secure the loose areas of the weaving on the front of the shirt, cut small pieces of Stitch Witchery or fusible web to slide under the strips. Then press to fuse on top of the woven area (Fig. 11).

6 Carefully turn the shirt inside out. On the wrong side of the shirt, check to see that the weaving lines are straight and that the horizontal strips are not pulled too tightly, or too loosely. Slide your hand under the shirt front to remove the pins on the sides of the weaving.

7 Cut a piece of lightweight fusible interfacing slightly larger than the weaving area and fuse it to the wrong side of the shirt over the weaving (Fig. 8). Then pin a larger piece of tear-away stabilizer over the weaving and interfacing.

8 Turn the sweatshirt right side out. With thread to match the sweatshirt, sew along the sides of the weaving, stitching close to the edge of the vertical cut lines (Fig. 9). Sew on the sides of some of the vertical and horizontal rows (Fig. 10). This stitching will be hidden and serves to stabilize the design. Remove the stabilizer after stitching.

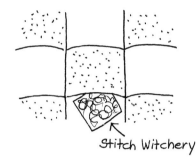

FIGURE 11. To hold the loose woven areas in place, slide a small piece of Stitch Witchery under the strips. Fuse in place.

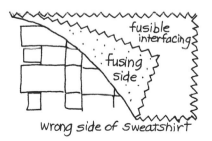

FIGURE 8. Fuse lightweight fusible interfacing to the back side of the weaving to hold it in place. Hint: Cut the interfacing with pinking shears so the edges will not be obvious on the right side of the shirt.

FIGURE 9. Sew along the right and left sides of the weaving area to secure the layers of fabric.

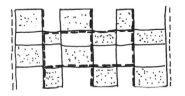

FIGURE 10. Add extra stitching on the lines inside the weaving.

9 Be sure to turn the sweatshirt inside out before laundering. This will help protect the woven area. It's also a good idea to wash this shirt by hand, though I tested woven designs in the washer and dryer, and they turned out well after laundering.

Find another fleece-cutting project for the sweatshirt front in Buttons and Bows on page 116.

✦ RELAXED WEAVING ✦

Relaxed weaving adds style to this shirt. Remember, you don't have to limit yourself to the designs in this project. Experiment with different trims and designs, and let your own preferences guide you.

Using a relaxed, loose weave, I added torn fabric strips to the front and sleeves of this sweatshirt. For another dimension to the design, I also added a miniature doily and ribbons. (The fabrics I used were all from P & B; the miniature doilies were from Wimpole Street Creations.)

 ## Supplies Needed

- assorted strips of fabrics
- ¼ yd. (23cm) paper-backed fusible web (or a narrow roll to speed up cutting)
- one sweatshirt
- clear nylon thread

- ½ yd. (46cm) stabilizer (optional)
- buttons, fabric yo-yos, miniature doilies, or other trim

1 Begin by tearing fabric strips for your design. Tear across the grain (Fig. 1). On the sweatshirt photographed, the ten strips were each 15″ (38cm) long or ⅓ the width of 45″ (114cm) fabric. Make yours any length you want. You might also tear them in different widths. I suggest that you tear no narrower than 1″ (2.5cm) strips as the tearing action distorts fabrics in narrower widths. Tear more strips than you think you'll use. It's nice to have extras and a variety of colors or prints for experimentation.

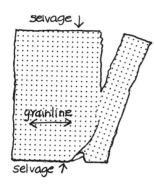

FIGURE 1. Tear strips of fabric for weaving across the grain of cotton fabric.

2 Cut away the loose threads on each fabric strip and also cut off the selvage ends (Fig. 2). Press the strips on both sides of the fabric. As you select the strips to use in your design, fuse a strip of paper-backed fusible web on the center of the wrong side (Fig. 3).

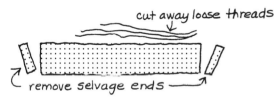

FIGURE 2. Cut away the selvage ends and loose threads and then press each strip of fabric.

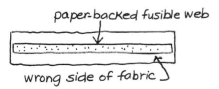

FIGURE 3. Fuse a piece of paper-backed fusible web to the wrong side of each strip.

3 With the sweatshirt placed flat on a table or board and the front side facing up, begin pinning strips horizontally or diagonally (Fig. 4). Pin one end of each strip to the sweatshirt on the right side and then proceed to weave the additional strips through the secured strips. Leave gaps in the weaving to show the sweatshirt or weave with the edges of all strips meeting. Turn under the ends of each strip and vary the lengths, as I have done on the sweatshirt illustrated (Fig. 5).

FIGURE 4. Place the fabric strips directly on the sweatshirt to plan the arrangement.

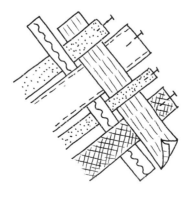

FIGURE 5. Weave additional strips of fabric through the strips pinned to the shirt and turn under the ends of all the strips.

4 After you have planned your design, fuse it carefully to the sweatshirt. Plan to sew around several of the inside strips to secure the entire woven unit to the shirt. Pin the centers of each inside strip section you plan to sew. Then pin down the ends of each strip. (Trust me on this—you'll never regret using all those pins!) (Fig. 6).

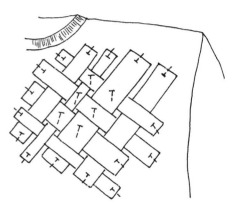

FIGURE 6. After fusing the strips to the shirt, pin all ends in place and also a section in the center.

5 Carefully turn the sweatshirt inside out. It will be easier to sew this large design to the shirt with the bulk of the shirt above your work rather than beneath it (Fig. 7).

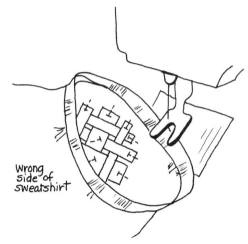

Wrong side of sweatshirt

FIGURE 7. The easiest way to work on the sweatshirt and sew the fabric strips is to turn the shirt inside out first.

6 Use clear nylon thread as top thread and a neutral color in the bobbin to blend with all the fabric colors you've chosen. Set the machine to sew a narrow zigzag stitch to catch the torn fabric edge as you sew.

7 Though I did not use a stabilizer with this project, you may prefer to have one beneath the stitching and on the wrong side of the sweatshirt front.

8 First sew around the edges of the inner strip sections marked by pins (Fig. 8). Then sew around the entire outside edge of the design. For a hidden stitch on the folded ends of the strips, catch the edge of the

fabric as the needle swings to the left. On the right swing of the zigzag, the needle stitches only through the sweatshirt (Fig. 9). Keep a small pair of sharp scissors handy to trim away the loose threads from the fabric strips.

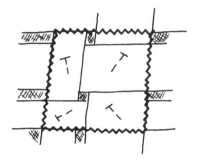

FIGURE 8. Use a zigzag stitch and clear thread to sew around the center sections of the woven design.

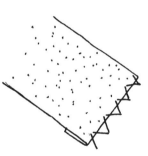

FIGURE 9. The zigzag stitch at the strip ends catches and secures the folded edge of the fabric.

9 Press the design area on the wrong and right sides of the sweatshirt. Add buttons, fabric yo-yos, or other trim to the design, as shown on the shirt in the photo.

10 Use leftover fabric strips to trim the sweatshirt sleeve or sleeves. Cut open

the stitching on the sleeve seam, opening it nearly to the end of the seam. Select fabric strips for the weaving, add paper-backed fusible web to the wrong sides, and plan the design directly on the opened sleeve (Fig. 10). Trim away excess length on the strips, turn under the edges, and pin. As with the shirt front design, sew around one or more of the inside strip sections and then around the entire design. Press the design and then sew or serge the sleeve seam closed again.

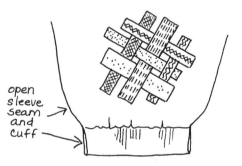

open sleeve seam and cuff

FIGURE 10. Open the sleeve seam and cuff to lay the sleeve end flat to arrange and sew the woven design. Afterwards, sew the seam closed again.

There are lots of options with this design project. Use bias-cut fabric strips instead of torn strips for a "thread-free" edge. Other alternative strips are ribbon, lace, and fabric strips with serged edges. For a quilted look to the design, sew down the center of each strip.

For another fun, creative weaving project, try Life's a Party on page 127.

✦ COOL AND UNUSUAL STRIPES ✦

For my nontraditional stripes, I chose a variety of fabrics and trims and manipulated them into a diagonal formation. Search through your sewing room for additional clever stripe choices. If you question whether any of your stripe materials are washable, test a piece by prewashing before you sew.

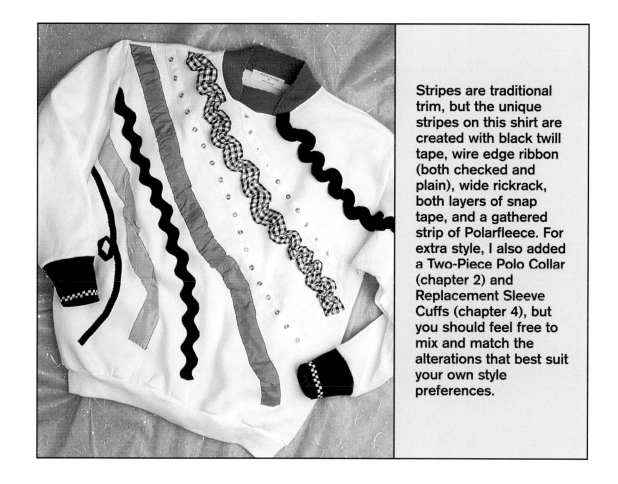

Stripes are traditional trim, but the unique stripes on this shirt are created with black twill tape, wire edge ribbon (both checked and plain), wide rickrack, both layers of snap tape, and a gathered strip of Polarfleece. For extra style, I also added a Two-Piece Polo Collar (chapter 2) and Replacement Sleeve Cuffs (chapter 4), but you should feel free to mix and match the alterations that best suit your own style preferences.

 ## Supplies Needed

- one sweatshirt with set-in sleeves
- assorted braids and trims, such as wire edge ribbon,

Polarfleece strips, extra-wide rickrack, twill, and snap tape

- 1 yd. (91.5cm) tear-away stabilizer
- clear nylon thread
- small piece of lightweight fusible interfacing (optional)

1 Plan the stripe layout on your sweatshirt. Use the diagonal design on the shirt photographed for ideas, plan your own diagonal design, or try something different. Plan to have extra ribbon extending past the neckline, shoulder, or sleeve seams as you'll tuck the stripes into the seamlines. If you are changing the shirt's neckline, staystitch around the neckline and remove the ribbing, using the instructions on pages 6–7. Then, sew on the stripes before re-doing the neckline.

2 You may want to try sewing wire edge fabric ribbon on clothing. It's easy to tuck and gather the edges into a position that stays—and you don't need gathering threads (Fig. 1). Position and pin the ribbon to the shirt in a straight or curving pattern. Another option is to fold the ribbon and angle it in a line across the shirt (Fig. 2). Turn under and pin the edge at the bottom of the ribbon.

Wire edge ribbon as straight or curved stripes

FIGURE 1. Bend the edges of wire ribbons to curve a stripe, or use the ribbon straight.

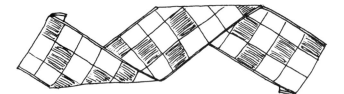

FIGURE 2. Wire ribbon folded at angles to create a unique stripe effect. Ends of ribbon are turned under before stitching.

3 The wide rickrack and each half of the snap tape are simply pinned to the sweatshirt, again with extra length at the shoulder or sleeve seam and the bottom edges are turned under (Fig. 3). Keep in mind: The cut ends of wide rickrack ravel easily.

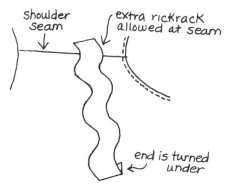

shoulder seam

extra rickrack allowed at seam

end is turned under

FIGURE 3. Allow extra length for wide rickrack and snap tape so the ends can be inserted in the shoulder seamline.

4 Gather the ribbons or a 1″ (2.5cm) strip of Polarfleece for an interesting dimensional stripe. On the wire edge ribbon I sewed with a long stitch diagonally from side to side. On the Polarfleece I stitched as illus-

trated with 6 stitches in each direction (Fig. 4). After sewing, pull on the bobbin threads to gather the ribbons or fabrics. For an invisible gathering seam on multicolor ribbon, use clear nylon thread. Pin the gathered stripes to the sweatshirt using many pins.

FIGURE 4. To gather a strip of Polarfleece, sew six stitches in each direction. Then pull the gathering threads.

5 On this project, I found it easiest to turn the sweatshirt inside out carefully and sew from the bottom ends of the ribbons to the tops. Use a stabilizer under the sweatshirt front and attach it before sewing on the stripes. Attach all strips using clear nylon thread and a straight or narrow zigzag stitch. Use bobbin thread to match the sweatshirt color. When sewing the snap tape, use the zipper foot and stitch close to the edge of the tape on both sides (Fig. 5).

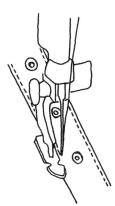

FIGURE 5. Use a zipper foot to sew the edges of snap tape.

Sew to the top of each stripe and stop stitching close to the shoulder or sleeve seams or to the neckline where the end of the stripe will be inserted (Fig. 6).

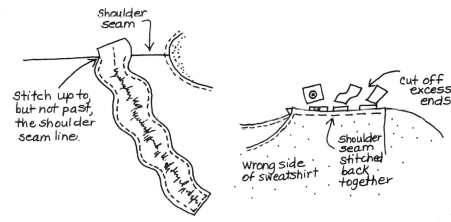

FIGURE 6. Sew all the way up to the shoulder seamline.

6 After sewing the stripes to the shirt, remove the stabilizer and carefully cut open the shoulder and sleeve seams in the areas where the loose ends need to be inserted (Fig. 7). On the wrong side of the sweatshirt, stitch the seams closed again and cut off the excess stripe fabrics (Fig. 8).

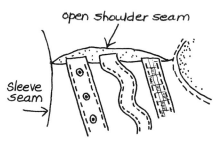

FIGURE 7. Open the shoulder seam so you can insert the stripe ends.

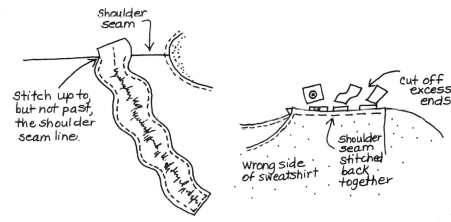

FIGURE 8. After sewing the shoulder seam closed, cut off the extra fabric from each stripe.

7 If the ends of the wire edge ribbons stick through the fabric, tuck the wires into the seam allowance. To prevent the ribbon from scratching whoever wears the sweatshirt, fuse a piece of lightweight fusible interfacing over the ribbon ends (Fig. 9).

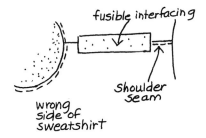

FIGURE 9. Fuse a piece of interfacing to the ribbon ends.

8 Press the sweatshirt from the back and the front. Pay attention to the iron temperature and the types of fabrics you're pressing. If the iron is too hot, it could ruin the wire ribbons or other fabrics that you've used.

The challenge I gave myself for this shirt was to use nontraditional fabrics and trims. See Mary's Miscellaneous Trim Ideas on page 115 for more unusual stripe choices.

✦ SPONGE PAINTING AND STITCHING ✦

The artistic effect produced by applying paint to a sweatshirt with a sponge is easy to create. You don't have to have the talent of Picasso or Van Gogh to add this unique painting feature that almost looks like an applique.

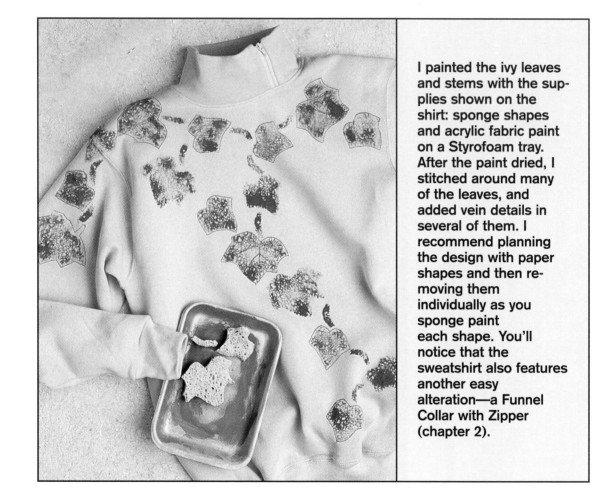

I painted the ivy leaves and stems with the supplies shown on the shirt: sponge shapes and acrylic fabric paint on a Styrofoam tray. After the paint dried, I stitched around many of the leaves, and added vein details in several of them. I recommend planning the design with paper shapes and then removing them individually as you sponge paint each shape. You'll notice that the sweatshirt also features another easy alteration—a Funnel Collar with Zipper (chapter 2).

 ## Supplies Needed

- one light-colored sweatshirt
- large piece of cardboard to slide inside shirt
- household sponges to cut into design shapes
- fabric paint
- paint tray or disposable surface, such as tin foil or a styrofoam meat tray
- paper towels
- small pieces of fabric for testing sponge painting
- ¼ yd. (23cm) tear-away stabilizer

1 Make sure to wash the sweatshirt before sponge painting. Prepare the shirt by sliding a large piece of cardboard inside (Fig. 1). It will serve as a firm surface for pressing the sponges on the shirt and also will prevent the paint from reaching the back of the sweatshirt. Add extra pieces of cardboard into the sleeves if you'll be painting on them as I did on my shirt.

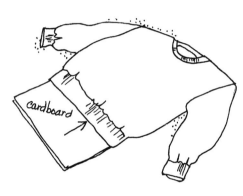

FIGURE 1. A piece of cardboard inside the shirt will absorb paint coming through the fabric and serve as a firm surface for pressing sponges on the sweatshirt.

Ivy leaves and stem for sponge or applique patterns

FIGURE 2. Ivy leaves and stem.

2 The next task is to plan the design and where you will press the paint-covered sponge "appliques." The best suggestion is to cut the chosen design shapes, such as the Ivy Leaves and Stem (Fig. 2), from colored paper. Cut several of each shape so you can experiment and lay out various arrangements (Fig. 3). Once the arrangement is set, you can leave the paper patterns in place and move them out of the way one at a time as you sponge paint each shape.

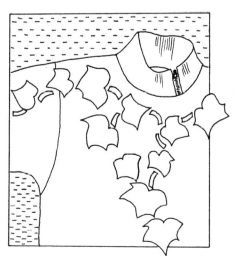

FIGURE 3. Plan a design with paper copies of the patterns you will cut from the sponges.

3 Place the paper design shapes on a sponge, trace around the edges, and cut them out (Fig. 4). Naturally, simple shapes will be easier to cut.

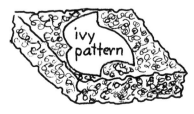

ivy pattern

FIGURE 4. Trace and cut the paper design shapes from a sponge.

4 Pour fabric paint onto a disposable surface, such as a large piece of tin foil or a Styrofoam meat tray from the grocery store. Spread the paint out to an area large enough for the size of the sponge shapes. Lightly press the sponge surface into the paint. Rub the painted surface on an open area of the paint tray to distribute the paint. Test the sponge by pressing it on a paper towel. This will get rid of excess paint. Then test the sponge on an extra piece of fabric.

Not enough paint or too much? You'll quickly get the "feel" of how hard to press on the sponge to transfer the paint. Remember two things: (1) Practicing a few sponge presses on paper towels and fabric will give you all the experience and courage you'll need to paint on the sweatshirt, and (2) Not every painted shape has to look the same or look perfect.

5 Remove the paper shapes you laid out on the sweatshirt as you press the paint-covered surface of the sponge at each location. This way you can avoid tracing each shape on the shirt.

6 Allow the paint to dry for 24 hours. Then remove the cardboard. Press the sweat-

shirt or follow the instructions for fabric painting that came with the paint. At this point you can be done with the sweatshirt, but for an extra artistic touch, I recommend sewing around all or some of the painted shapes.

7 For a noticeable stitching line around the painted designs, use what I call a "repeater" stitch, one that goes back and forth (Fig. 5). On my sweatshirt I used Sulky rayon thread to match the paint color. Make sure to have a stabilizer under the areas where you sew.

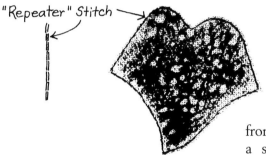

FIGURE 5. Sew around sponge painted shapes for a more distinct outline. A heavier, repeating stitch is a good choice.

8 Some of the ivy leaves have veins stitched in the centers. (Fig. 6). I sewed these

lines without a pattern, but if you'd feel more confident, draw some lines with a chalk marker or a washable marking pen before you sew.

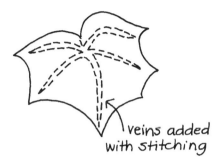

FIGURE 6. For extra detail, sew lines inside the leaves to suggest veins.

Another option you have with sponge painting is to paint with a sponge on a plain piece of fabric and then cut appliques from the fabric and sew them to a sweatshirt. But don't stop there. Let you imagination and creativity be your guides. Experiment with paint, sponges, and accent stitching—and see what decorating ideas you can come up with.

✦ MITTEN GALLERY ✦

Frame a collection of appliqued mittens with a running stitch and continue the stitching to trim the circle neckline, sleeves, and bottom hem.

For this wintry shirt, I chose soft fabrics, such as knits and Polarfleece, for the mitten appliques and used a running stitch and black crochet thread to frame and separate the mittens. Artificial snowflakes sprinkled around the shirt echo the snowflakes in the facing fabric.

Supplies Needed

- assorted "warm-looking" fabrics, such as thermal knit, knit velour, Polarfleece, sweatshirt fleece
- ¼ yd. (23cm) paper-backed fusible web
- one sweatshirt with set-in sleeves

- 6″ (15cm) of braid trim
- ½ yd. (46cm) stabilizer
- clear nylon thread
- two buttons for mitten with overlap

- 12″ (30.5cm) of narrow ribbon for connecting mitten pair
- black crochet thread and embroidery hand sewing needle
- beeswax (optional)

1 Trace the mitten shapes on page 114 onto paper-backed fusible web. Remember to trace two of the Small Mittens and reverse the direction of the second one (Fig. 1).

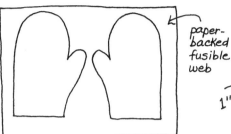

FIGURE 1. Trace two of the smallest mitten shapes on paper-backed fusible web. Flip the design over for the second mitten so the thumb points in the opposite direction.

2 Fuse the mitten shapes to the wrong sides of fabric you have chosen. (One exception: I used the fleecy side of sweatshirt fabric as the right side on the tan mitten.) Cut out the mittens. On the Snowflake Mitten, cut out the design through the paper backing and fabric. Use small sharp scissors or straight edge and round eyelet buttonhole cutters (Fig. 2).

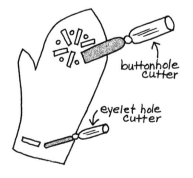

FIGURE 2. Cut the snowflake design with buttonhole and eyelet hole cutters.

3 For the Ruffled Mitten, gather and sew a 1" x 5" (2.5 x 12.5cm) strip of fused fabric to the bottom edge of the mitten. Cut off any excess ruffle fabric (Fig. 3). Fuse decorative braid on the Small Mitten pair. Turn under the braid ends (Fig. 4).

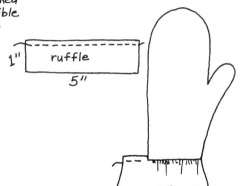

FIGURE 3. Gather a 1" x 5" strip of fabric with paper-backed fusible web applied to the wrong side. Insert it under the bottom edge of the mitten. Cut off any excess ruffle length before fusing the mitten and ruffle to the shirt.

FIGURE 4. Fuse the ends of decorative braid to the wrong sides of the pair of small mittens.

4 Remove the paper backing from all the mittens and set them aside while you prepare the frame on the shirt.

5 Cut out a piece of paper 12" x 11" (30.5 x 28cm). I taped together two pieces of typing paper to get a large enough piece for the pattern. As noted on the illustration, cut notches in the edges to indicate where the inside lines will be drawn (Fig. 5).

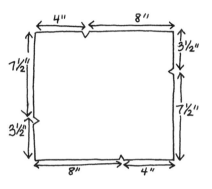

FIGURE 5. Cut a paper pattern for the outline of the mitten gallery frame. Cut notches at the points marked on the diagram.

6 With a chalk marker or washable marking pen, mark the center front of the shirt, using the directions on page 5. Place and pin the paper outline on the sweatshirt, centering it on the front (Fig. 6). Try on the shirt to check the placement. Trace around the edges, marking the notched areas. Remove the paper, and measure and connect the lines, as illustrated (Fig. 7).

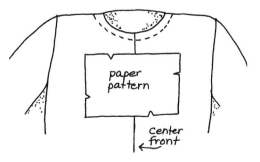

FIGURE 6. Pin and trace the outline on the shirt front with a washable marking pen.

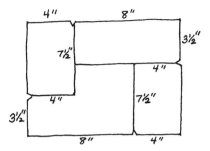

FIGURE 7. Draw and connect the lines from the notches to complete the gallery division lines.

7 Now place the mitten appliques inside the frame and fuse them to the shirt. For the Snowflake Mitten, you may want to have the sweatshirt color show through or place extra fabric, as I did, beneath the cut areas before fusing (Fig. 8). Form a pleat in the wide-bottom edge of the Pleated Mitten before fusing it to the shirt (Fig. 9).

FIGURE 8. For a two color mitten, place extra fabric under the holes cut into the snowflake mitten.

FIGURE 9. Fold a pleat into the bottom edge of the wide mitten before you fuse it to the shirt.

8 Stitch the edges of the mittens to the sweatshirt using stabilizer underneath on the wrong side of the shirt. Use clear nylon thread and a very narrow zigzag or blanket stitch to catch the edges (Fig. 10).

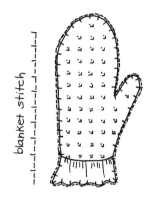

FIGURE 10. Try stitching around the mittens with clear thread and a blanket stitch for a nearly invisible attachment.

9 You can add a running stitch around the mittens for further trim (see Step 10 for directions). Sew two buttons on the overlapped edge mitten (Fig. 11). Draw a line from one Small Mitten to the other one and sew ribbon to the line or satin stitch along it to form the mitten cord.

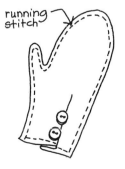

FIGURE 11. Trim the tucked edge mitten with two buttons and a contrasting thread running stitch.

10 Next, remove the stabilizer and hand sew the mitten gallery frame. Thread a sharp embroidery needle with one or two strands of black crochet thread. Pull the thread through the openings in the beeswax opener to coat it and keep it from tangling (Fig. 12). The running stitch is easy and fun to do. This could be a television watching project. Don't worry about each stitch being perfect; just sew. After every few stitches, pull slightly on the fabric and thread to make sure you're not sewing too tightly. All the knots go on the back side of the sweatshirt.

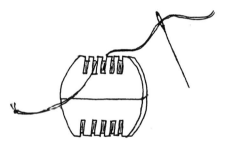

FIGURE 12. Run the handsewing thread across beeswax to keep it from tangling.

I removed the ribbing from the collar, cuffs and bottom edge of my sweatshirt and then finished the edges with facings (see pages 9–10). I then added detail to the shirt's neckline, sleeves, and hem by trimming them with the running stitch.

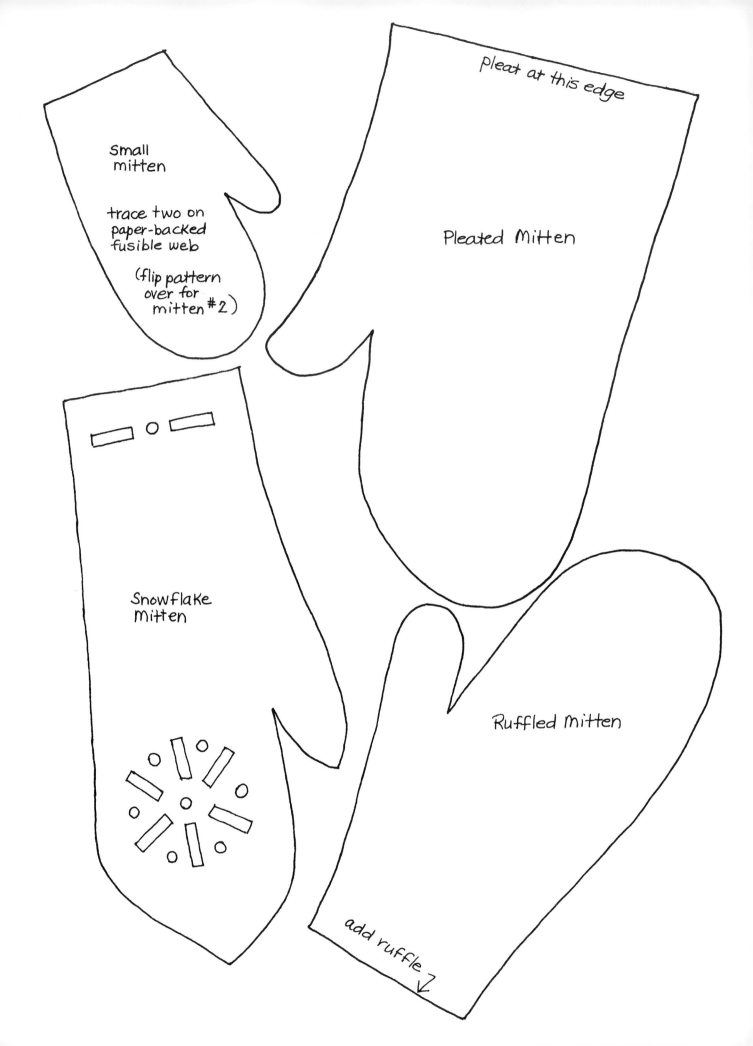

small
mitten

trace two on
paper-backed
fusible web

(flip pattern
over for
mitten #2)

pleat at this edge

Pleated Mitten

Snowflake
mitten

Ruffled Mitten

add ruffle

Mary's Miscellaneous Trim Ideas

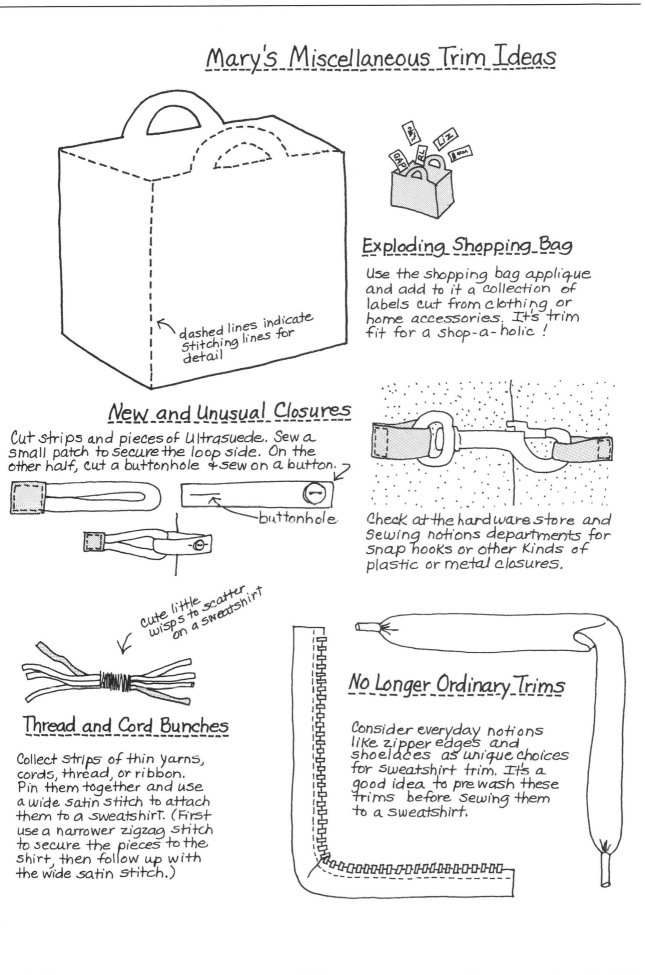

← dashed lines indicate stitching lines for detail

Exploding Shopping Bag

Use the shopping bag applique and add to it a collection of labels cut from clothing or home accessories. It's trim fit for a shop-a-holic!

New and Unusual Closures

Cut strips and pieces of Ultrasuede. Sew a small patch to secure the loop side. On the other half, cut a buttonhole & sew on a button.

buttonhole

Check at the hardware store and sewing notions departments for snap hooks or other kinds of plastic or metal closures.

Cute little wisps to scatter on a sweatshirt

Thread and Cord Bunches

Collect strips of thin yarns, cords, thread, or ribbon. Pin them together and use a wide satin stitch to attach them to a sweatshirt. (First use a narrower zigzag stitch to secure the pieces to the shirt, then follow up with the wide satin stitch.)

No Longer Ordinary Trims

Consider everyday notions like zipper edges and shoelaces as unique choices for sweatshirt trim. It's a good idea to prewash these trims before sewing them to a sweatshirt.

✦ BUTTONS AND BOWS SWEATSHIRT ✦
by Marilyn Gatz

Coordinating fabric, buttons, and thread combine to create this attractive decoration. Notice that you can easily vary the widths of the rectangles and gather the top and bottom edges in alternating rectangles for a different look.

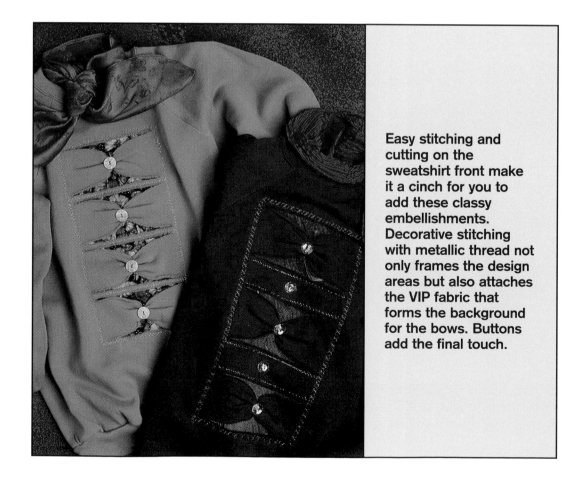

Easy stitching and cutting on the sweatshirt front make it a cinch for you to add these classy embellishments. Decorative stitching with metallic thread not only frames the design areas but also attaches the VIP fabric that forms the background for the bows. Buttons add the final touch.

Supplies Needed

- one sweatshirt
- ¼ yd. (23cm) of print fabric for backing of design area
- ¼ yd. (23cm) lightweight fusible interfacing
- Sulky Sliver (metallic) thread
- four to six decorative buttons

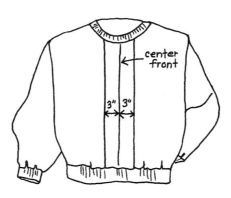

FIGURE 1. Mark the shirt's center front and then draw a line 3″ away on each side of the center line.

1 With a chalk marker or washable marking pen, mark the center front of the sweatshirt, as described on page 5. Draw two lines parallel to the center front 3″ (7.5cm) on each side (Fig. 1). Beginning 3″ (7.5cm) below the center front neck edge, draw perpendicular lines to intersect the two parallel lines. Line two will be 3″ (7.5cm) from the first line, line three will be 2″ (5cm) down from there, line four 3″ (7.5cm) down from there, and so on. Continue as far down the shirt as you want to place the bows (Fig. 2).

FIGURE 2. Draw horizontal lines across the three vertical lines at 3″ and 2″ intervals.

2 Measure the design area that you've drawn on the front of the sweatshirt, and cut a piece of print fabric slightly larger than that. Prepare the fabric by interfacing it with lightweight interfacing. With the right side of the fabric facing the wrong side of the shirt, pin the fabric to the front of the shirt (Fig. 3).

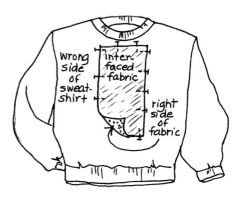

FIGURE 3. Interface the wrong side of a piece of fabric larger than the shirt front's design area and pin it in place on the wrong side of the shirt beneath the ruled off design area.

3 Stitch on all the lines 3″ (7.5cm) below the neckline, except the center front line, which was used as a gauge only. You'll sew through the sweatshirt and the print fabric. Use a decorative stitch and metallic thread for an extra decorative touch.

4 After the stitching is complete, carefully cut a horizontal line through the front shirt fabric just inside the stitching of each 3″ (7.5cm) rectangle (Fig. 4). Bring the top and bottom edges together at the center and hand or machine stitch the gathered fabric together through the fabric layer. Sew the button over the center. You can place additional buttons on each strip between bows for an extra special touch (Fig. 5).

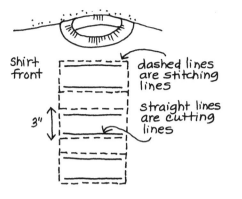

FIGURE 4. Cut a horizontal line at the top and bottom edge of each 3″ rectangle stitched into the shirt. Make sure you're cutting through the sweatshirt layer only.

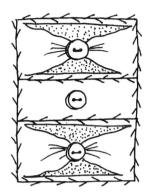

FIGURE 5. Gather the centers of the cut areas together and secure with a button. Add extra buttons to the uncut 2″ rectangles.

✦ ELEGANT BEADED SWEATERSHIRT ✦
by Nancy Bednar

Nancy was inspired by the beautifully tailored and embellished clothing from the 1930s and 40s and transferred her ideas to this sweatshirt. The designer label added to the shirt's back neckline further personalizes this one-of-a-kind "sweatershirt."

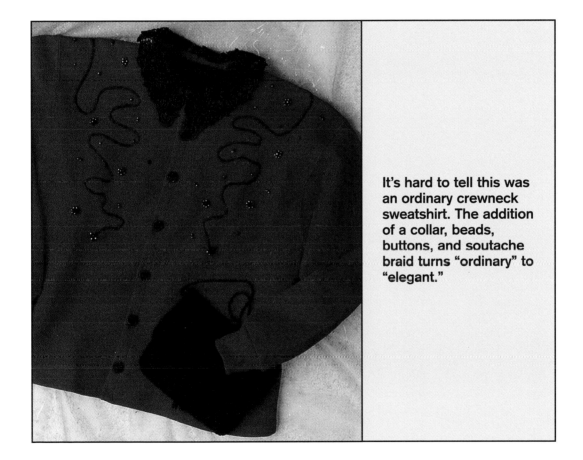

It's hard to tell this was an ordinary crewneck sweatshirt. The addition of a collar, beads, buttons, and soutache braid turns "ordinary" to "elegant."

Supplies Needed

- one sweatshirt with set-in sleeves one size larger than is normally worn
- 3–5 yds. (3–5M) 1" (2.5cm) wide grosgrain ribbon to match the sweatshirt color
- two packages of soutache braid
- one two-part Venetian or Battenberg lace premade collar
- seam sealant
- six to eight buttons $5/8"$ (1.5cm) diameter
- beads in assorted sizes for embellishing

➤Note: Venetian collars, Battenberg lace collars, and soutache braid only come in a limited number of colors, but you can easily dye white ones to a color of your choice with hot water dye, such as Rit, or cold water dye, such as Dylon.

1 Using a chalk marker or washable marking pen and the steps on page 5, mark the center front of the sweatshirt. Staystitch ¼" (6mm) on each side of the center front line and cut open the sweatshirt, using the instructions on page 6. Remove the bottom band of ribbing to create a boxier jacket-style sweatershirt as explained on page 7.

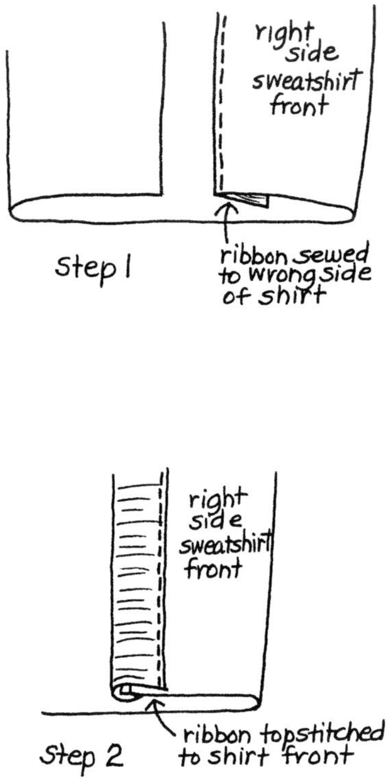

2 To finish the center front edges, sew 1" (2.5cm) wide grosgrain ribbon as follows, using a scant ¼" (6mm) seam allowance: For the right side (as you look at the sweatshirt), sew the ribbon to the wrong side of the sweatshirt, flip to the right side. Topstitch down (Fig. 1). For the left side, sew the ribbon to the sweatshirt front edge, turn to wrong side and topstitch down along the unstitched edge (Fig. 2).

3 Finish the bottom edge of the sweatshirt by sewing ribbon to the right side of the sweatshirt, pressing, turning under, and topstitching down to the wrong side (Fig. 3).

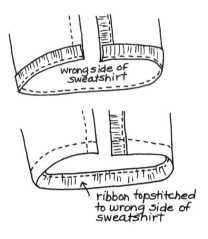

FIGURE 3. Sew ribbon to the sweatshirt bottom edge by first sewing it to the right side of the shirt, then turning it to the wrong side and topstitching to hold it in place as the sweatshirt hem facing.

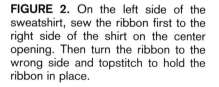

FIGURE 1. To finish the right side of the sweatshirt front edge, sew 1" grosgrain ribbon to the wrong side of the shirt. Then turn the ribbon to the right side of the shirt and topstitch in place.

FIGURE 2. On the left side of the sweatshirt, sew the ribbon first to the right side of the shirt on the center opening. Then turn the ribbon to the wrong side and topstitch to hold the ribbon in place.

4 On the left and right sides of the sweatshirt, draw asymmetrical squiggles with your chalk marker or washable marking pen. Be sure to extend the design lines to the back of the shirt for continuity (Fig. 4).

FIGURE 4. With a washable marking pen, draw curved, swirling lines on the left and right sweatshirt fronts.

5 Sew soutache braid to the sweatshirt following the lines you drew. If you prefer a thicker braid for a bolder look, as shown on the shirt in the photo, zigzag together two pieces of soutache and sew down using a 2.0 double needle.

6 Pin the two collar parts to the inside top edge of the neckline ribbing. You will probably overlap edges at the center back. Straight stitch in place and flip the collar over to the right side (Fig. 5).

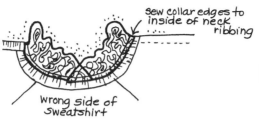

FIGURE 5. Sew the collar pieces to the inside of the neck ribbing and then flip the collars to the right side of the shirt.

7 Mark the left (as you're looking at the shirt) center front of the sweatshirt for six to eight buttonholes, as desired. Eliminate the need for a button-

hole through the neckline ribbing by using a hook and eye (Fig. 6). Sew the buttonholes, coat them with seam sealant, and cut them open when totally dry. Sew the buttons on the right side.

FIGURE 6. Sew a hook and eye to the neckline of the sweatshirt to eliminate a button and buttonhole.

8 Turn your sweatshirt into a "sweatershirt" by embellishing the front and back with beads. Sew on as few or as many as you'd like. Enjoy being a "Sweater Girl" of the 90s!

✦ FLATLOCK FRENZY ✦
by Jenny Osborn

Here's a great way to show off some of your favorite fabrics. A simple geometric design translates into a classy wearable.

Fabric strips cut and serged together with the flatlock technique form the yoke for this sweatshirt. The original neck ribbing was removed and then reattached after the yoke was sewn in place.

 ## Supplies Needed

- one sweatshirt with set-in sleeves
- ¼ yd. (23cm) of three 100% cotton fabrics

- wax paper
- ½ yd. (46cm) lightweight fusible interfacing

- decorative serger thread
- ¼ yd. (23cm) paper-backed fusible web

1 Cut 1½"-2" (4-5cm) wide strips of each of the three cotton fabrics, cutting across the fabric from selvage to selvage. Cut enough strips so that you will have some for practice and then to piece a block of fabric approximately 12" x 45" (30.5 x 114cm). Determine the placement of the fabric strips.

2 Set the serger for the widest three-thread flatlock and use decorative thread (YLI Pearl Crown Rayon or Decor Six are suggested) in the upper looper, with standard thread in the needles and lower looper. Make necessary adjustments for flatlocking, as described in your serger manual. With wrong sides together, serge a test strip. "V's" should form on the back of the fabric with the upper and lower looper meeting on the edge (Fig. 1). Skim the edges as you stitch and then pull the fabrics open to flatten the stitches. If your machine has a two-thread capability, set up for a two-thread flatlock with decorative thread in the lower looper and standard thread in the needle.

FIGURE 1. For a flatlock stitch, "v's" form on the back of the fabric with upper and lower looper threads meeting at the fabric edges.

3 With wrong sides of the strips together, continue serging as described above until a piece of fabric is created that is approximately 12" x 45" (30.5 x 114cm).

4 Remove the sweatshirt's neck ribbing using the instructions on pages 7–8. Also, using a chalk marker or washable marking pen, mark the shirt's center front line, as explained on page 5.

5 Create a template for the serged fabric by drawing the yoke directly on the shirt to determine the proper placement and size. Measure down at the center front of the shirt 6" (15cm) from the neck edge; this will be point A. Next, measure

4" (10cm) down on the sleeve seam from the shoulder for point B. Draw a line connecting points A and B (Fig. 2).

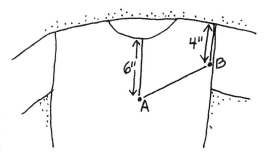

FIGURE 2. Draw the yoke shape on the shirt by measuring and marking and connecting points A and B.

6 Place a piece of wax paper over the sweatshirt and trace with the end of the seam guide to mark the outline of the yoke area onto the paper. Add a ½" (1.3cm) seam allowance to the center front (Fig. 3).

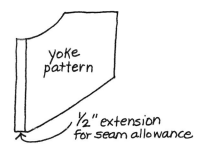

FIGURE 3. Extend the center front edge of the yoke pattern by ½" to add a seam allowance.

7 Fold the right sides of the serged fabric together, aligning the strips and pinning the two layers together. Place the yoke template on the fabric so that the longer, bottom side of the yoke is on the center of a strip (Fig. 4). The center front will be on an angle. Cut out the yoke. Staystitch around each piece of the yoke to prevent ravelling.

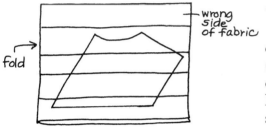

FIGURE 4. Position the yoke pattern on the wrong side of the folded, serged fabric, placing the bottom edge of the yoke in the center of a strip.

8 Cut out two pieces of interfacing using the yoke template minus the extra seam

allowance at the center front. Fuse the interfacing to the wrong sides of the yoke pieces.

9 Using a three-thread stitch, serge the bottom edges of the yoke pieces with decorative thread in the upper looper and standard thread in the needles and lower looper. Thread the extra tails of serging through the stitching on the back side of the yoke with a double-eyed needle.

10 With wrong sides together, flatlock the center yoke seam with a ¼" (6mm) seam allowance. (The extra ¼" of the ½" seam allowance is the leeway provided so the yoke fits well on the shirt.) Lay the yoke on the sweatshirt to double-check the size. Serge the shoulder and side edges with a three-thread decorative serging stitch. You won't need to serge the curved neckline edge because it will be covered by the new neckline or collar.

11 To prepare to attach the yoke to the shirt, fuse strips of paper-backed

fusible web to the wrong side ¼" (6mm) from the edges (Fig. 5). Fuse the yoke in place on the sweatshirt front. Next, straight stitch the yoke to the sweatshirt, sewing over the serged edge stitching with matching thread. Trim the neck edge at this time, if necessary.

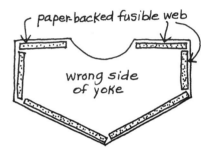

FIGURE 5. Fuse strips of paper-backed fusible web to the edges on the wrong side of the yoke.

12 Sew or serge on the neck ribbing that you removed earlier, or fashion a new neckline with one of the techniques from chapter 2 of this book.

✦ SOME BUNNY SWEATSHIRT ✦
by Janis Giblin

This fast-and-easy sweatshirt trim uses decorator hotpads found in home linen departments. Use one with a bunny to achieve the look of this sweatshirt, or choose another design that catches your fancy.

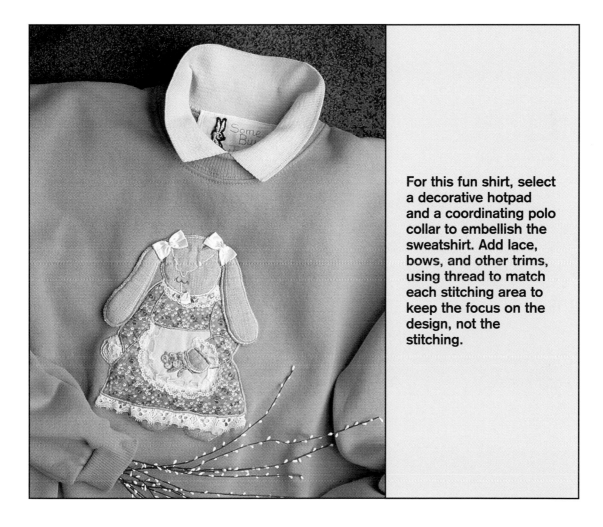

For this fun shirt, select a decorative hotpad and a coordinating polo collar to embellish the sweatshirt. Add lace, bows, and other trims, using thread to match each stitching area to keep the focus on the design, not the stitching.

Supplies Needed

- one polo/finished-edge knit collar
- one sweatshirt
- one decorator hotpad
- assorted ribbon roses and trims to embellish hotpad

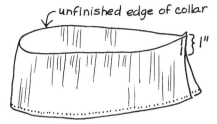

FIGURE 1. Sew the two ends of the collar together, stitching down 1″ from the unfinished edge and close to the collar end edges.

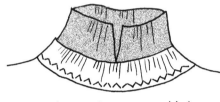

right side of sweatshirt

FIGURE 2. Zigzag stitch the collar to the shirt neckline by sewing on the shirt's neck ribbing. Use a thread color to match the shirt.

1 Sew the ends of the polo collar together, stitching from the unfinished edges about 1″ (2.5cm) (Fig. 1). Using a chalk marker or washable marking pen, mark the quarter portions on both the collar and the sweatshirt neckline, as directed on page 8. Sew the collar to the neckline with a zigzag stitch, sewing on the right side of the sweatshirt above the lower edge of the ribbing (Fig. 2).

2 Cut the hanging loop from the hotpad as well as any loose threads. Bartack ribbon roses or other trim to the hotpad.

3 Check the stitching on all areas of the hotpad and restitch if edges are not well covered with thread.

4 Position and pin the hotpad with its trim about 2½″ (6.5cm) below the shirt's center front neckline ribbing (Fig. 3). Try on the sweatshirt to test the placement. Using a medium width (3.0) zigzag stitch, sew around all the edges of the hotpad.

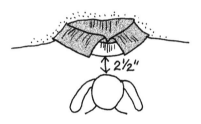

FIGURE 3. Place the hotpad or other trim 2½″ below the ribbing and try the shirt on to test the placement.

You'll enjoy searching for new and interesting hotpads for sweatshirts—hotpads too cute to get dirty in the kitchen.

✦ Life's A Party Sweatshirt ✦
by Kelly Harlow

Bright colors, beads, and eyelets look almost like streamers on this fanciful shirt. Using Ultrasuede for the ribbon adds texture.

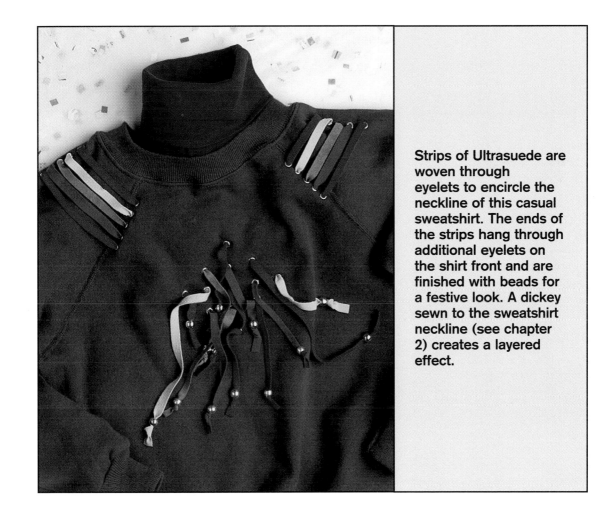

Strips of Ultrasuede are woven through eyelets to encircle the neckline of this casual sweatshirt. The ends of the strips hang through additional eyelets on the shirt front and are finished with beads for a festive look. A dickey sewn to the sweatshirt neckline (see chapter 2) creates a layered effect.

 ## Supplies Needed

- one sweatshirt with raglan sleeves
- ¼ yd. (23cm) fusible tricot knit interfacing

- eyelet punch or Prym Vario snap setter
- seam sealant
- size 13 tapestry hand sewing needle

- five (6mm) strips of Ultrasuede 45″ (114cm) long or five (6mm) ribbons 45″ (114cm) long
- lightweight beads for strip ends (optional)

1 Using a chalk marker or washable marking pen, mark the center front, center back, and shoulder lines of the sweatshirt. Use the instructions on page 5 as a guide.

2 With the right side of the shirt facing up, mark the eyelet row positions. Place one row of eyelets 1″ (2.5cm) from the neck ribbing of the sweatshirt: (1) below the shoulder seam on each side of the neckline and (2) below each raglan seam on the front and back of the shirt (Fig. 1).

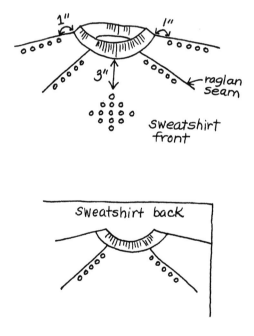

FIGURE 1. Eyelet placement markings at raglan seams, shoulder lines, and center front of the sweatshirt neckline.

Position the center front eyelets in a diamond shape 3″ (7.5cm) down from the center front neckline (Fig. 2). Space the eyelets ½″ (1.3cm) apart in the rows at the shoulders and raglan sleeves.

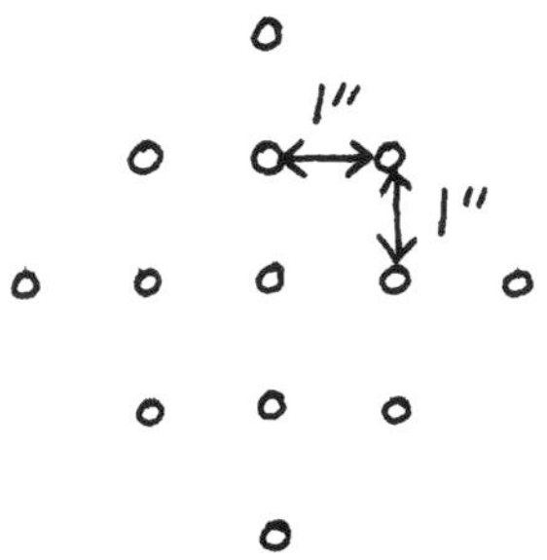

FIGURE 2. On the wrong side of the shirt, fuse interfacing strips beside the raglan seams (shirt front and back), at the shoulder lines, and also a 5″ square beneath the center eyelet motif.

3 On the wrong side of the shirt: Fuse 1″ x 5″ (2.5 x 12.5cm) strips of interfacing to the marked eyelet rows at the shoulder and raglan seams. At center front, fuse a 5″ (12.5cm)

square of interfacing to the diamond shape, matching up the interfacing with the top and bottom points (Fig. 3).

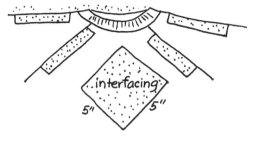

FIGURE 3. Thirteen eyelets are placed 1″ apart in five rows to form a diamond shape.

4 Using an eyelet tool or a Prym Vario snap setter, punch the eyelets into the sweatshirt on the right side, being careful not to stretch the fabric and pull the eyelets out.

5 On the wrong side of the fabric, reinforce each eyelet with a drop of seam sealant. Wait for this to dry before lacing the eyelets.

6 Cut ¼" (6mm) strips of Ultrasuede or use ribbons for the lacing strips. For an adult size small, the 45" (114cm) width of the fabric yielded strips of exactly the right length. For longer strips, simply knot off on the wrong side of the sweatshirt and start a new strip as needed.

7 With the right side of the sweatshirt facing up, use the tapestry needle to thread the strips through the eyelets: Thread a ¼" (6mm) strip in through one of the center front eyelets, pull it out through one at the raglan seam, in through the one at the shoulder seam, and so on around the neckline until the strip is pulled out through an eyelet in the center front (Fig. 4). Be careful not to tug on the eyelets and pop them out of the shirt. Continue this process with the remaining four strips.

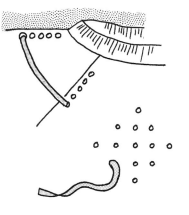

FIGURE 4. Start each strip in one of the center front eyelets, pass the strip on the wrong side of the shirt through an eyelet at the raglan seam, and then into an eyelet at the shoulder. Continue weaving to the back of the shirt and around to the front and bring the strip through another center front eyelet.

8 When all the strips have been threaded, three empty eyelets will remain in the center front. Cut three 8" (20.5cm) strips of Ultrasuede and thread them through the empty eyelets, knotting on the wrong side to secure them to the sweatshirt. Finish the ends the same as the other strips.

9 The strips will form an attractive yoke effect around the shirt neckline. Finish the ends of the strips by adding beads (and knotting the ends to hold the beads in place) or by knotting the ends of all or some of the strips.

Kelly recommends laundering this shirt in a mesh lingerie bag or pillowcase on a gentle cycle in cold water. Lay it flat to dry.

✦ TRIO OF TRILLIUM ✦
by Barb Prihoda

On this shirt, the trillium shapes are traced onto nylon organdy, embroidered with free-motion straight stitch, cut out of the organdy, and used as a thread applique on the sweatshirt. Framing strips and an added collar complete the shirt.

Trillium are one of Barb's favorite spring flowers. By the time they bloom in the spring, Minnesotans know that winter is really over. She used the basic trillium shape from my Minnesota Applique Designs folder and enlarged it. With free-motion machine embroidery she was able to add extra detail to the flowers. Look closely to see the designer's initials at the bottom of the design and also on the label inside the neck. Be sure you sign your sewing creations too!

Supplies Needed

- three 9" (23cm) squares of white nylon organdy
- 6"–7" (15–18cm) wooden machine embroidery hoop
- fine point permanent pen (Pigma)
- 40 weight rayon machine embroidery thread in these colors: dark grey, dark green, light green, dark pink, medium pink, white
- lightweight white cotton thread for bobbin
- ¼ yd. (23cm) paper-backed fusible web
- 12" (30.5cm) medium yellow 4mm silk ribbon
- machine embroidery needles
- small amount of fiberfill for trapunto stuffing
- button front chambray shirt with collar (consider using a shirt that is worn or the wrong size or style since you will be using only the collar area)
- scrap piece of denim a little darker than the chambray shirt
- ½" (1.3cm) wide bias tape maker (optional)
- iron-on tear-away stabilizer

1 All of the embroidery for this project uses a free-motion straight stitch. Keep the following points in mind when setting up and beginning this type of sewing.

- Drop or cover the sewing machine feed dogs.
- Replace the regular press foot with a darning foot.
- Set the machine for a straight stitch, with a zero stitch length.
- Put in a new machine embroidery needle (size 75 or 90).
- Use a bobbin filled with white lightweight cotton thread.
- Thread the top of the machine with 40-weight rayon thread.
- Loosen the top tension 1–2 numbers or notches.
- Hoop the fabric "drum tight" in a wooden *machine embroidery* hoop.
- Bring bobbin thread to the surface by taking one complete stitch, hand turning the sewing machine wheel.
- *Put the presser foot lever down.* This is a very important step to avoid knotted masses of thread at the bottom of your work.
- Lock on the threads by taking a few stitches in place.
- Do some practice stitching on an extra piece of fabric to "warm up."

2 To begin the trillium design, place one organdy square in the hoop. Be sure it is "drum tight." Place the hoop and organdy over the trillium design in the book (Fig. 1) and trace it with a fine point permanent pen. Include the arrows in your tracing.

FIGURE 1.
Trillium flower pattern.

3 Follow Figure 2 for color placement. All embroidery is done using a straight stitch to fill in the areas. Use the arrows to determine the proper stitch direction. Fill in the areas completely, but smoothly. Do not overfill: This makes it more difficult to embroider, the threads will fray, and the embroidery will look bumpy.

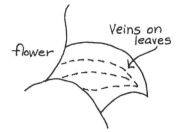

FIGURE 3. Straightstitch the lines for veins inside each leaf.

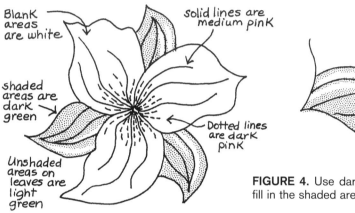

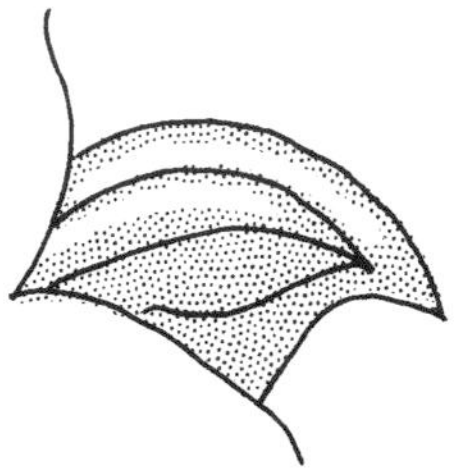

FIGURE 2. Flower illustration for color placement.

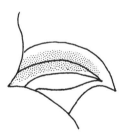

FIGURE 4. Use dark green thread to fill in the shaded areas on each leaf.

4 Stitch the leaves first. Begin by straight stitching the veins with dark grey. Go over each line at least twice (Fig 3). Use dark green to outline each leaf. Go over each line 2–3 times. Fill in the shaded areas (Fig. 4), following the directional arrows in Figure 1. Change to light green thread and finish filling in the leaves. Blend the light green into the dark green (Fig. 5). Go over the dark grey veins again if you have covered them too much.

FIGURE 5. Stitch in the shaded area with light green thread and blend with dark green stitching.

5 To stitch the flower, begin with dark pink thread and straight stitch along the dotted lines near the center of the flower (Fig. 6). Change to the medium pink thread. Outline each petal, stitching over each outline twice, and stitch the veins inside the petals, indicated by the solid lines of the design.

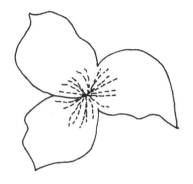

FIGURE 6. With dark pink thread, stitch the dotted lines in the flower center.

6 Use white thread to fill in the petals with straight stitching, following the directional arrows. It is okay to go over the pink lines somewhat as this will blend them into the white. Try not to cover them completely and do not overfill them with the straight stitching. You want the petals to have a smooth look to them.

7 When the embroidery is completed, remove the organdy from the hoop and fuse a square of paper-backed fusible web slightly larger than the design to the wrong side of the fabric. Cut out the design leaving a ⅛″ (3mm) margin around the embroidered areas (Fig. 7). Repeat these steps for the other two trillium.

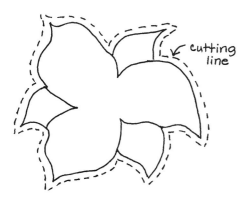

FIGURE 7. Cut the embroidered flower with a ⅛" border around the entire design.

8 Iron a piece of stabilizer to the wrong side of the sweatshirt front. Use a piece large enough to cover the area that will include the chambray and denim strips. Try on the shirt to plan the placement of flowers. Using a chalk marker, washable marking pen, or pins, mark on the shirt where you want them to go. Then, fuse them to the shirt, using a press cloth. Fuse the leaves securely, but only lightly fuse the petals as you will need to separate the petals from the sweatshirt later to do the trapunto stuffing.

9 Cut open one side seam of the sweatshirt, or remove the stitching. If there are no sideseams, cut the shirt open along one side where the sideseam would be, stopping your cutting line about 1" (2.5cm) below the underarm seam.

10 To attach the edges of the embroidered designs to the sweatshirt, use a

free-motion straight stitch to embroider over and cover the raw edges of the design. It will look as if you did all the embroidery directly on the sweatshirt. Use a darning foot and thread to match the area of the design you are going to embroider—for example, dark green around the leaves and medium pink around the flowers. You do not need to use a hoop for this because you will not be doing heavy embroidery, and you have the iron-on stabilizer helping to hold the fabrics flat. Straight stitch on the raw edge of the organdy, again following the direction of the stitches. Blend your stitches into the already embroidered petal or leaves, securing the applique completely (Fig. 8).

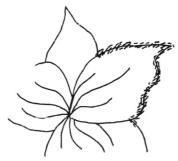

FIGURE 8. With thread to match the flower area you are attaching, blend the stitches into the embroidered edges.

11 As you stitch around the petals, continue the stitching into the very center of the flower (Fig. 9). This will make each petal separate when you do the trapunto stuffing.

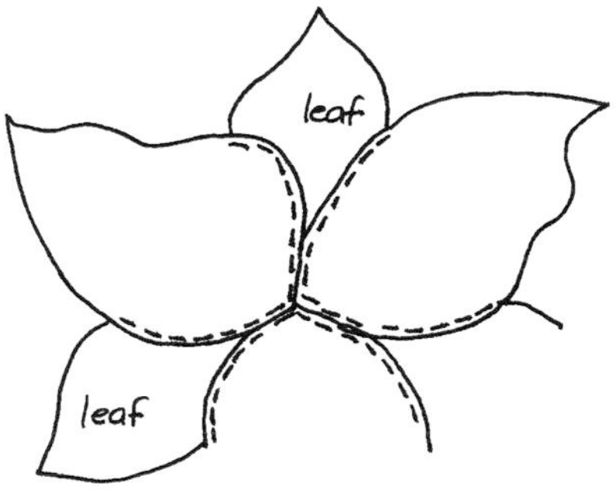

FIGURE 9. Dotted lines indicate stitching to center of flower to define petal shapes.

12 When the embroidery /applique is finished, remove the stabilizer only from behind the trillium. Pull on the center of each petal to separate its fusing from the sweatshirt. Carefully make a 1" (2.5cm) slit in the sweatshirt fabric directly behind each petal. Use a small flat tool like a wooden point turner to finish separating the fused areas. Place a small amount of fiberfill into this slit, into the petal. Once it is evenly stuffed, hand whipstitch it closed (Fig. 10).

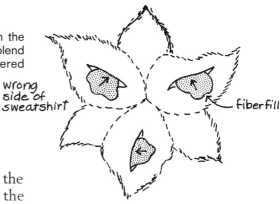

FIGURE 10. Lightly stuff fiberfill into the back of each flower petal and then handstitch to close the slit in the sweatshirt back.

13 Use the 4mm yellow silk ribbon to make six stamens in the center of each flower. Do a narrow lazy daisy stitch by hand (Fig. 11).

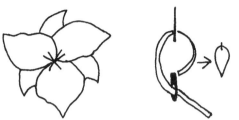

FIGURE 11. Add six stamens to flower center by handstitching with 4mm yellow silk ribbon.

14 The next addition to the sweatshirt is the collar. You will need to use a button front shirt (men's or women's) with a collar. Use the collar of a shirt that has seen some use but may be a little out of style or is now the wrong size. Check at the consignment store, using the consignment shopping tips in *Mary Mulari's Garments with Style*. The collar needs to fit (although you can always wear it open) and not show serious signs of wear. The fabric from the body of the shirt can also be used to trim the sweatshirt—it's a perfect match. The button front shirt will be changed into an attached dickey that is sewn to the back neckline of the sweatshirt but hangs loose in the front. It can be worn buttoned or unbuttoned and fits over the head easily.

15 Lay the button front shirt flat on a table, matching front to back, with the shoulder line at the top. Using a chalk marker, a washable marking pen, or pins, mark the shoulder lines. Since many shirts have a yoke instead of an actual shoulder seam, you need to mark where the shoulder seam would be if there were one (Fig. 12).

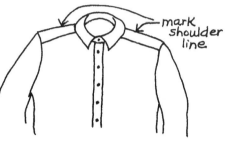

FIGURE 12. Mark the shoulder line on each side of the shirt neckline.

16 Cut the dickey shape out of the shirt, front and back together, with the cutting lines 3" (7.5cm) out from the neckline seam on the shoulder lines and 6" (15cm) down from the center front of the shirt (Fig. 13). Round out the lower corners. Clean finish by turning under the edge and sewing or serging the front of the dickey from shoulder line to shoulder line. Leave the back edge unfinished as it will be cut off and discarded.

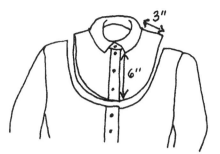

FIGURE 13. Mark 3" from each side of the neckline and 6" down from the shirt's center front and cut the dickey shape from the shirt.

17 Pin the back neck seam of the collar to the back neck seam of the sweatshirt, right side of the collar to the wrong side of the sweatshirt. Match the shoulder lines of the collar piece to the shoulder seams of the sweatshirt. Stitch in the ditch of the sweatshirt back neckline seam, with the sweatshirt right side up. Sew from one shoulder seam to the other (Fig. 14).

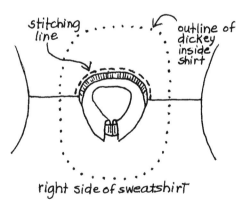

FIGURE 14. With the dickey pinned inside the sweatshirt, stitch in the ditch of the sweatshirt back neck seam.

18 Trim the excess fabric from the back of the dickey about ¼" (6mm) from the stitching line. Trim from shoulder line to shoulder line. Leave the front of the dickey 3" (7.5cm) wide at the shoulder seam area (Fig. 15). Fold the raw edge of this extension under, and then stitch in the ditch on the shoulder seam, catching the folded edge, to secure the dickey. Cover the raw edge of the collar along the back neckline seam with a piece of bias tape made from the excess shirt fabric (Fig. 16).

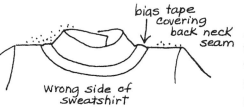

FIGURE 16. Sew a piece of bias tape (cut from the excess shirt fabric) over the dickey collar's back neck seam.

19 Use the excess fabric from the shirt, along with a slightly darker piece of denim, to make a partial frame for the lower corner of your trillium design. This sets off the design nicely, and ties the chambray collar in with the whole sweatshirt. Cut from the excess shirt fabric, on the straight of grain, one piece 11½" x 1" (29 x 2.5cm) and one piece 11" x 1" (28 x 2.5cm). From the darker denim, on the straight of grain, cut one piece 10½" x 1" (26.5 x 2.5cm) and one piece 9½"x 1" (24 x 2.5cm). Fold and press the long edges to the center of each piece. Use the bias tape maker if you have one. Fray the short ends of each piece about ¼" (6mm) (Fig. 17).

20 Fuse strips of paper-backed fusible web to the wrong sides of each strip and then fuse the strips to the sweatshirt using the diagram as a guide and weaving the corner. Use the blanket stitch on your sewing machine to sew the strips in place (Fig. 18). Remove the stabilizer from the back of the shirt and sew up the side seam.

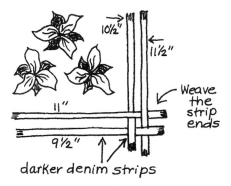

FIGURE 18. Weave the ends of the four strips to form a corner frame for the three flowers. Fuse in place and sew with a blanket stitch.

Identify your work with a special "designer" label and wear your Trio of Trillium sweatshirt with pride.

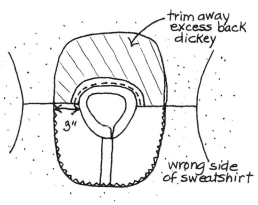

FIGURE 15. Cut away the extra fabric on the back of the dickey, leaving 3" at each shoulder line.

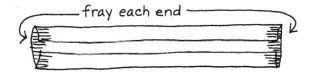

FIGURE 17. Fray the ends of the bias strips.

✦ Shaped-Up Sweatshirt ✦
by Steph Barry

Coordinating fabric does more than decorate in this shirt—it adds a cinched waist and slimmed-down sleeves.

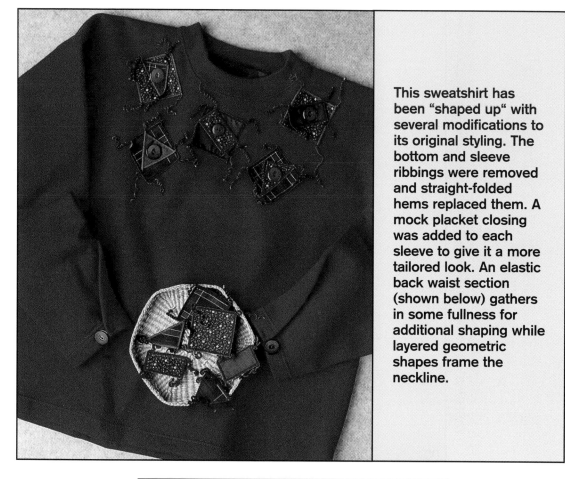

This sweatshirt has been "shaped up" with several modifications to its original styling. The bottom and sleeve ribbings were removed and straight-folded hems replaced them. A mock placket closing was added to each sleeve to give it a more tailored look. An elastic back waist section (shown below) gathers in some fullness for additional shaping while layered geometric shapes frame the neckline.

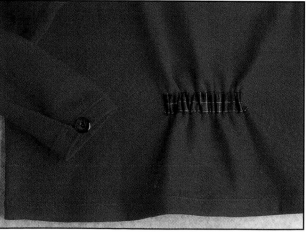

Supplies Needed

- one sweatshirt
- one double needle for the sewing machine
- 12" (30.5cm) piece of 1" (2.5cm) wide elastic
- seam sealant
- ⅛ yd (11.5cm) of two or three fabrics
- scrap of Ultrasuede, 1" x 1" (2.5 x 2.5cm)
- ¼ yd. (23cm) lightweight fusible interfacing
- woolly nylon thread to coordinate or contrast with fabrics
- seven buttons (five for layered shapes and two for cuffs)
- bodkin or large safety pin for threading elastic

1 Remove the bottom ribbing from the sweatshirt and press and straighten the bottom edge, using the instructions on pages 7 and 12. Turn under the bottom edge and pin in place. Sew around the hem with a double needle (Fig. 1).

FIGURE 1. Sew a hem around the sweatshirt bottom with a double needle.

2 Remove the ribbing from each sleeve and press and straighten the bottom edges. Turn under the bottom edges and pin in place. Sew around to hem with a double needle, as with the sweatshirt bottom hem. To stabilize the fabric before pinning and stitching, fuse a strip of paper-backed fusible web to the hem, turn under the bottom edge and fuse the hem to the shirt, and stitch with the double needle.

3 The mock sleeve placket has a loop of elastic thread which slips around the button and allows the opening to stretch wider, without unfastening the button, when you slide your hand in and out. Try on the sweatshirt to determine where the button should be located on the outside of your wrist. Mark the location with a chalk marker, washable marking pen, or pins. Also measure the amount of fabric that needs to be tucked so the sleeve fits more closely to your wrist size. Make sure the "placket" folds down to the button (Fig. 2).

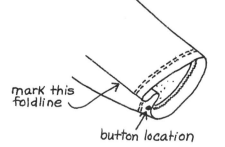

FIGURE 2. Mark the button location and the tuck foldline.

4 Use the rolled-hem stitch on your serger to cover the elastic thread for the button fastener so it will match your sweatshirt. Set the serger for a balanced rolled hem stitch (stitch length 1.0, stitch width 1.5). First, unroll 15"–20" (38–51cm) of elastic and position it on the bed of the serger so the elastic is to the right of the needle and to the left of the blade. Hold the elastic somewhat taut so it feeds straight through and avoids being nicked by the cutting blade. Serge over a section of elastic about 8" (20.5cm) long. Then add a drop of seam sealant at one end of the thread-covered elastic. Measure about 2" (5cm) down and add another drop of sealant. Add a third drop of sealant another 2" (5cm) down (Fig. 3). Allow the seam sealant to dry; then cut at each drop location to get two 2" (5cm) elastic segments to be used for button loops.

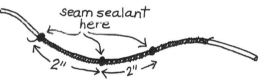

FIGURE 3. Place three drops of seam sealant at 2" intervals on the serged elastic.

5 Fold the 1" (2.5cm) square of Ultrasuede in half. Fold each 2" (5cm) elastic piece into a loop. Position the ends of the elastic pieces inside the folded Ultrasuede (Fig. 4). Stitch back and forth across the end of the Ultrasuede to secure the loop ends. Then cut the fabric between the loops to create the two loop sections.

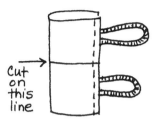

FIGURE 4. Place the ends of the elastic loops inside the folded Ultrasuede piece and stitch on the fabric edges. Then cut the fabric in half to make two button loops for the sleeves.

6 To determine where you will fold your placket, use the excess sleeve width that you measured earlier. To create the placket, fold the second pin mark to meet the button pin mark (Fig. 5).

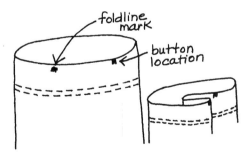

FIGURE 5. Meet the foldline and button marks.

7 To attach the loop, fold the bottom of the sleeve at the second pin mark and place one loop section near the hem edge so the loop extends past the folded edge. The loop section can be attached to either side of the fold, depending on whether you want to see the Ultrasuede patch on the outside of your placket or prefer to have it concealed on the inside. Sew the Ultrasuede square to the folded sweatshirt sleeve to secure the loop section to the shirt (Fig. 6).

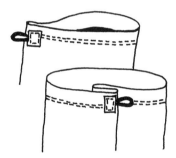

FIGURE 6. Sew each Ultrasuede loop piece to the folded sleeve.

8 Sew the button on each sleeve at the button location. Slip the elastic loop around the button to finish the cuff treatment.

9 The next step is the gathered waist casing. Keep in mind that you can vary the length of the rectangle and elastic based on the fit you want and the fullness of the sweatshirt. Cut a 3″ x 8″ (7.5 x 20.5cm) rectangle of fabric. Fold the fabric in half

along the long side with right sides together. Sew the three sides using a ¼″ (6mm) seam allowance and leaving a 2″ (5cm) opening to turn the fabric. At each end of the opening, pivot the stitching from the seamline and sew to the edge of the fabric to make the opening turn neatly to the inside. Turn the rectangle right side out (Fig. 7).

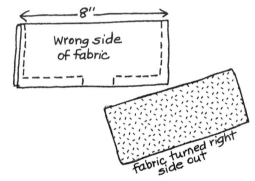

FIGURE 7. Leave a 2″ opening in the waist casing to turn the fabric right side out.

10 Mark the center line of the back of the sweatshirt, using the directions for finding the center front line on page 5. Try on the sweatshirt and mark your waistline. Center the fabric casing on the center back line and place the upper edge along the waistline marking (Fig. 8). You can place the rectangle on the outside of the sweatshirt for a decorative look or on the inside where it will not show. Edge stitch along the top and bottom edges of the rectangle.

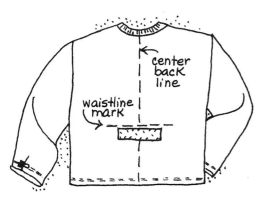

FIGURE 8. Place the fabric casing at waistline mark and centered on the center back line.

11 Place a mark 4″ (10cm) from one end of the 1″ (2.5cm) piece of elastic. Use a bodkin or safety pin attached to the end of the elastic to pull it through the rectangular casing.

12 Pull the elastic so the fabric rectangle on the first end just covers it, and pin in place. Stitch the short side of the rectangle closed. Just inside the straight stitching line, sew with a narrow zigzag stitch through the rectangle, elastic, and sweatshirt to hold the end in place. Then pull the elastic at the opposite end until you see the 4″ (10cm) mark (Fig. 9).

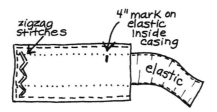

FIGURE 9. Secure the left end of the elastic to the casing and sweatshirt by stitching with a zigzag stitch.

Pin the elastic in place and trim off the extra length. Use a narrow zigzag stitch to secure this end of the elastic and then edge stitch the last side of the rectangle (Fig. 10).

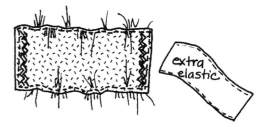

FIGURE 10. Gathered back waist casing with zigzag stitching on each end to hold elastic in place.

13 The final addition to the sweatshirt is the layered geometric shapes framing the shirt front neckline. I've included the patterns for the shapes in the book (Fig. 11). The shapes are made by serging two pieces of fabric with a narrow three-thread stitch, with

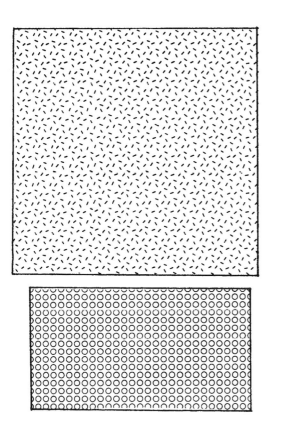

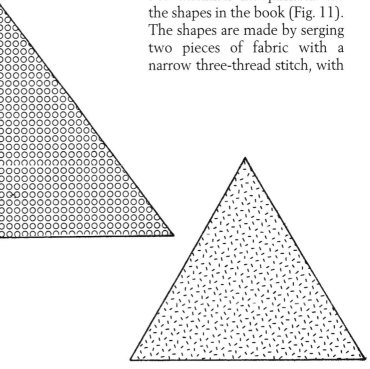

FIGURE 11. Geometric applique shapes for serging.

the thread tails left dangling from each corner. They are layered one on top of the other and secured to the sweatshirt with buttons. If you are using more than two fabrics, mix and match fabrics and shapes as you are cutting them out.

14 To give the shapes some stiffness, fuse interfacing to the fabric before you cut the shapes out. Cut 2½" x 22" (6.5 x 56cm) strips of each fabric to be used for the layered shapes. Cut 2¼" x 22" (6 x 56cm) strips of interfacing and fuse them to the wrong sides of each fabric strip.

15 Layer a front and back fabric strip with wrong sides together. Use a gridded ruler and rotary cutter or a template to cut out each shape through both layers of fabric. (You can recycle empty breakfast cereal boxes by using them for templates.)

16 Thread the serger with standard thread in the right needle and woolly nylon in the upper and lower looper in thread colors to match or contrast with the fabrics and sweat-

shirt. Use a narrow balanced three-thread stitch (stitch width 3.5, stitch length 1.5) to serge each side. Skim the edge of your fabrics as you are stitching and remember to leave long thread tails. If you want the thread tails to curl, don't pull the fabric away from the machine as it is making each tail.

17 Put a drop of seam sealant on each corner of the shape. Put another drop of seam sealant on each thread tail at whatever length you want (Fig. 12). Allow the sealant to dry and then clip off the extra thread length. If you don't want the thread tails, just apply sealant to each corner, let dry, and clip the thread at each corner.

FIGURE 12. Apply seam sealant at all four corners of the rectangle and also on the ends of the thread tails.

18 Arrange the shapes around the neckline. Place the square first; then choose a triangle or rectangle to layer on top (Fig. 13). Angle the second layer differently from the first. Place a pin in the center of each group of shapes. Try the sweatshirt on to check the placement. If you like the arrangement, stitch a button in the middle of each group to hold the shapes to the sweatshirt.

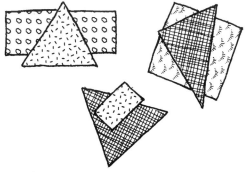

FIGURE 13. Combinations of layered geometric shapes.

Your "shaped up" sweatshirt now has decorations, mock sleeve plackets, and an elastic casing to shape the back. Enjoy wearing your work of alteration and art.

✦ FROM THE WILDS OF CANADA ✦
by Jan Saunders

"Go Wild" with this one-of-a-kind jacket. No one will guess that it was once a sweatshirt.

This sweatshirt was inspired by the fabric, a fine-pile 100% poly-animal "fur." The short cardigan is trimmed with detachable collar and cuffs (from Jan Saunders' Wardrobe Quick-Fixes) and paw prints appliques that track from front to back for walk-away interest. A machine-stitched designer label personalizes Jan's shirt and provides just the right the finishing touch.

Supplies Needed

- one sweatshirt in a bright or jewel-tone color with set-in sleeves
- ¼ yd. (23cm) color-coordinated lining fabric
- ½ yd. (46cm) animal print fabric
- five ½" (1.3cm) buttons
- ¼ yd. (23cm) interfacing (optional)

- one package black wide bias-cut hem facing tape
- ⅓ yd. (30.5cm) paper-backed fusible web
- one 12" x 14" (30.5 x 35.5cm) piece of black Ultrasuede
- glue-stick
- one 1½" (4cm) covered button set
- one pair of Velcro hook and loop "dots" or covered snaps

1 Remove the bottom ribbing of the sweatshirt using the instructions on page 7. Cut off the sleeves to a three-quarter length. Serge finish the raw edges of the sleeves and shirt bottom using the differential feed set from 1.5 to 2.0. Fold up a 1" (2.5cm) hem at the bottom and topstitch.

2 Mark the shirt's center front line with a chalk marker or washable marking pen, staystitch on each side of the line, and cut the shirt open along the center front line, using the instructions on pages 5 and 7.

3 Cut two long plackets, each 4" (10cm) wide across the grain and the length of the shirt front plus seam allowances. (For a thinner fabric, you may want to interface the fabric plackets.) Serge or zigzag one long edge of each placket piece. Sew the other long edges to the center front openings (Fig. 1). Turn the serged/zigzagged edges inside the shirt, making sure the edges extend past the stitching line. The placket width will be 1¾" (4.5cm). Pin in place and stitch in the "ditch" from the right side of the shirt (Fig. 2).

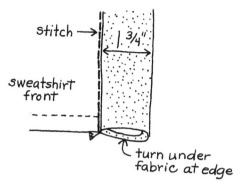

FIGURE 2. Stitch in the ditch to attach the zigzagged/serged placket edge to the sweatshirt.

4 Trace the Collar Pattern on page 145, and make sure to add ½" (1.3cm) seam allowances to all edges. Make the collar longer or shorter by adjusting the center back seam allowance (Fig. 3). Cut two top collar pieces from the animal print, two under collar pieces from the lining. Add interfacing if needed.

5 Seam the top and under collars at the center back. Press the seam allowances open. Tip: To work on faux fur, reduce the presser foot pressure, lengthen the stitch to 3.0–3.5 (6–9 stitches per inch), and sew with the fur side against the feed dogs.

6 With right sides together, seam the two collars together along the outside edges. With pinking shears, trim the seam allowance to within ¼" (6mm) of the stitching line. Turn the collar right side out. Then check to see that it fits around the neck edge of the sweatshirt.

7 Stitch the raw edges together, guiding ½" (1.3cm) from the edges. You may want to pull a little more of the undercollar fabric into the seam allowance so the lining won't show when the collar is on (Fig. 4). Serge finish the raw edge of the collar.

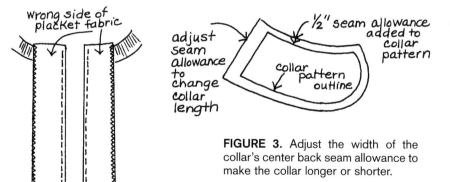

FIGURE 1. Sew the 4" wide placket strips to the open edges on the sweatshirt front.

FIGURE 3. Adjust the width of the collar's center back seam allowance to make the collar longer or shorter.

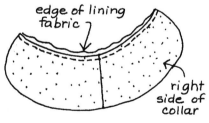

FIGURE 4. The lining fabric extends past the edge of the collar fabric so the lining will not show when the collar is worn.

8 Measure and cut a piece of hem facing tape the length of the serged edge of the collar plus ½″ (1.3cm) for seam allowances. Open hems of the tape. With right sides together, fold the tape in half lengthwise and seam both short ends using a ¼″ (6mm) seam allowance (Fig. 5). Turn the strip right side out. Press. Stitch five buttonholes for ½″ (1.3cm) buttons; they should be equidistant and parallel to the length of the tape (Fig. 6). Cut the buttonholes open.

10 Next, trim the sleeves with animal print cuffs. Measure around each sleeve end and add ½″ (1.3cm) for seam allowances. Cut two strips of cuff fabric to the measured length and 6½″ (16.3cm) wide. Serge finish the long edges of each strip.

11 Seam each cuff into a circle and press seam allowances open. Turn up and blind stitch a 1¼″ (3cm) hem on the edge of each cuff (Fig. 7).

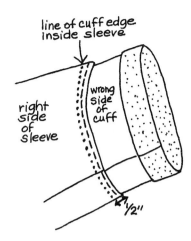

FIGURE 8. Sew cuffs to sleeve end with wrong sides of cuff and sleeve together.

FIGURE 5. Sew across both short ends of the folded tape.

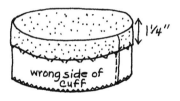

FIGURE 7. Cuff with 1¼″ hem hand-stitched in place.

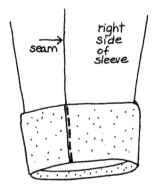

FIGURE 9. Fold the cuffs up on the right side of the sleeves and hold in place by stitching in the ditch of the cuff seam.

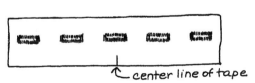

FIGURE 6. Mark and sew the first buttonhole at the center line of the tape.

12 Starting at the underarm seam, position each cuff on the sleeve with the wrong sides together, pinning the edge of the cuff ½″ (1.3cm) into the sleeve. Use the free arm on your sewing machine and sew with the shirt side up to attach each cuff to the sleeve (Fig. 8). To hold the cuffs in place, stitch in the ditch at the underarm seams (Fig. 9).

9 Place the raw edges of the tape on the neck edge of the collar and stitch a ¼″ (6mm) seam. Sew buttons to the inside of the neckband and button in the collar.

13 To add the paw print trim, trace the Paw Print Applique from the book (page 145) onto paper-backed fusible web. Flip the pattern over and trace four more sets. Fuse the paper to the wrong side of Ultrasuede and cut out the patterns. Remove the paper backing.

14 Position and temporarily glue-stick the paws, walking them on the front, over the shoulder, down the back, and on the sleeves, alternating left and right paws. Try on the shirt to check the placements. Fuse the prints to the shirt, using a press cloth to protect the fabric.

15 Cover a large, 1½″ covered button with an animal print scrap. Place the hook side of the Velcro fastener on the inside of the placket under where the button will be placed, and hand stitch the button and fastener at the top of the placket in one step. Hand stitch the loop side of the Velcro on the other placket (Fig. 10).

Don't forget to add your designer label. Jan stitched her name on a piece of Ultrasuede backed by a piece of stabilizer and attached it to a piece of the animal print. For other looks with this same sweatshirt, remove the collar or make contrasting collars.

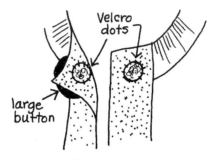

FIGURE 10. Sew Velcro to both sides of the placket opening.

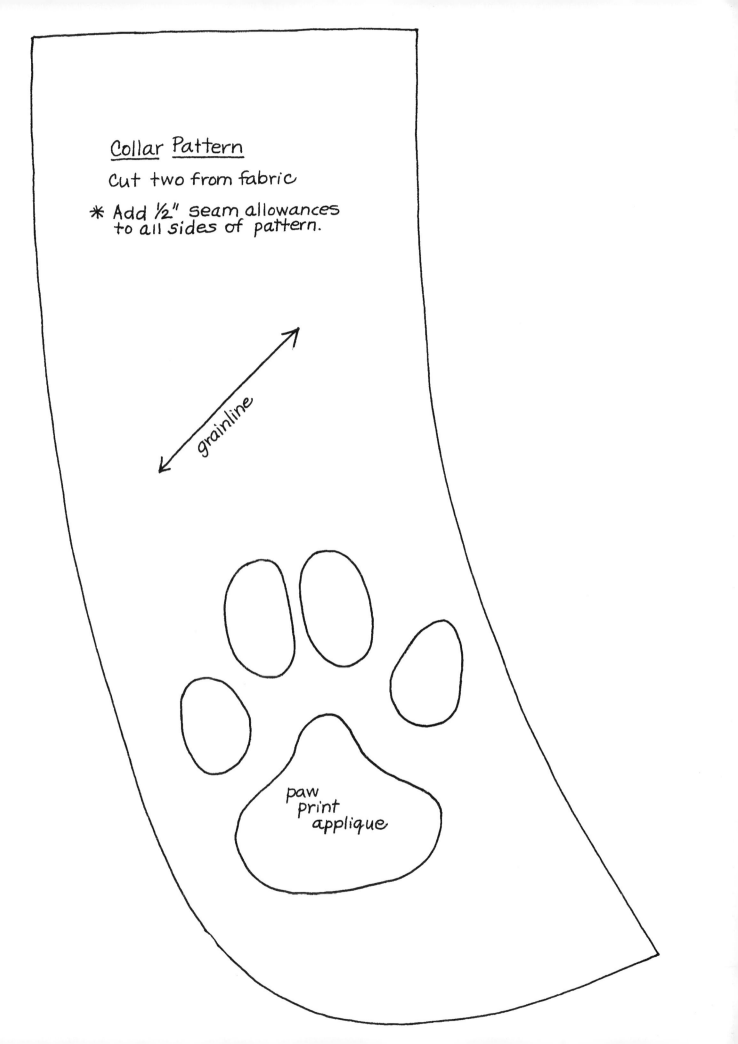

Collar Pattern

Cut two from fabric

* Add ½" seam allowances to all sides of pattern.

grainline

paw print applique

Cabin/Trees Applique Pattern

Applique design used on the sweatshirt on page 27.

Resources

I encourage you to check first locally for the availability of the fabrics and supplies required for the sweatshirt projects in this book. I strongly believe that sewing enthusiasts must support local retailers and help them stay in business so that their assistance, products, sewing knowledge, and sewing enthusiasm will continue to be available to us.

The following mail order sources are listed here to assist you in locating sewing supplies, blank sweatshirts, and other items listed in this book. If you contact any of the sources listed, please inform them that you learned of their products in *More Sweatshirts with Style* by Mary Mulari.

BARRETT HOUSE

P.O. Box 540585
North Salt Lake, UT 84054-0585
801-299-0700

Wimpole Street Creations products (miniature doilies, yo-yos, etc.) for sewing embellishment. Call or write for current information.

BODEK & RHODES

2951 Grant Avenue
Philadelphia, PA 19114
1-800-523-2721

Blank sweatshirts by mail order. Write or call for free catalog.

CLOTILDE

2 Sew Smart Way - B8031
Stevens Point, WI 54481-8031
1-800-772-2891

Sewing notions by mail order. Call or write for free catalog.

COLLARS & SHIRTS BY AUDREY

2033 Clement Ave., Ste. 217
Alameda, CA 94501-1313
1-800-336-7999

Polo collars & dickeys. Free mail order catalog.

GREAT COPY PATTERNS

Spiegelhoff's Stretch & Sew
P.O. 085329
Racine, WI 53408
414-632-2660

Great Copy patterns, sweatshirts, polo collars, & fabrics. Write or call for current information.

LANDS' END

1 Lands' End Lane
Dodgeville, WI 53595
1-800-356-4444

Blank sweatshirts & other fine quality clothing to decorate. Call or write for free catalog.

MARY'S PRODUCTIONS

Box 87-C3
Aurora, MN 55705

Creative sewing books, designs, & patterns by Mary Mulari. Send a self-addressed stamped envelope to receive current information.

ODDEN'S NORSK HUSFLID, INC.

Highway 63
P.O. Box 87
Barronett, WI 54813
715-822-8747

Pewter clasps and buttons for Nordic sweatshirt. Call or write for current information.

NANCY'S NOTIONS

P.O. Box 683
Beaver Dam, WI 53916
1-800-833-0690

Sewing notions & fabrics catalog. Call or write for free catalog.

STRETCH & SEW FABRICS

19725 40th Avenue West #G
Lynnwood, WA 98036
206-776-3700

Polo collars, fabrics, ribbing, & more. Send self-addressed stamped envelope or call for current information.

VANBERIA

217 West Water Street
P.O. Box 229
Decorah, IA 52101
1-800-628-5877

Pewter clasps and buttons for Nordic sweatshirt. Call or write for free catalog.

Behind the Readers' Gallery

BUTTONS AND BOWS SWEATSHIRT

After learning to sew for her family out of necessity, **Marilyn Gatz** has specialized in speed tailoring and altering designer ready-to-wear, machine arts, and fashion sewing. She is a former Stretch & Sew instructor and store manager. She currently presents sewing seminars around the United States. Her home is in Brookfield, Illinois.

ELEGANT BEADED SWEATERSHIRT

Since 1990, **Nancy Bednar** has been a writer for *Serger* and *Sewing Update Newsletter*. She also works as a freelance training consultant for Bernina of America and teaches at locations throughout the United States. An avid sewer since the sixth grade, she lives in La Grange Park, Illinois, with her husband, Ed, and children, Sarah and Adam.

FLATLOCK FRENZY

A sewer since age twelve, **Jenny Osborn** enjoys personalizing her garments using the serger and sewing machine. She resides in Mount Airy, Maryland, with her husband, Tim, and two pampered house cats. Jenny shares her love of sewing through involvement in the American Sewing Guild, teaching adults and children through local shops, and by judging the local 4-H Fashion Review each year.

SOME BUNNY SWEATSHIRT

At age five, **Janis Giblin** began to sew by hand. Sewing, needlework, and crafts have always been a part of her life. She has won over 200 ribbons at the Wisconsin State Fair. Her creations are worn by her husband, daughter, and mother, who cheer her on to greater projects. As she was encouraged to creative endeavors by her parents, she in turn encourages her kindergarten students to be creative. Janet lives in Oak Creek, Wisconsin.

TRIO OF TRILLIUM

Barb Prihoda is a registered nurse, but her sewing, embroidery, and desire to share these skills with others have taken the place of her nursing job. She now spends her time creating new designs and teaching machine embroidery. Her award-winning work has appeared in *Sewing Update Newsletter* and *The Creative Machine Newsletter.* She lives in Eagan, Minnesota, with her husband, Don, and her sons, Scott and Kyle.

FROM THE WILDS OF CANADA

For the past 22 years, **Jan Saunders** has shared her flair for fashion and her love for sewing with home sewers nationwide through her writing, teaching, and television appearances. She has authored/co-authored twelve books and has contributed to the *Update Newsletters, The Creative Machine Newsletter, Sew News,* and *Threads* magazines. She lives in Phoenix, Arizona, with her husband, Ted, and her son, Todd.

LIFE'S A PARTY

A wife and mother of two young children, **Kelly Harlow** also operates a multifacted sewing business, Heartland Design, from her home. She taught herself to sew in 1989 and now enjoys designing and creating one-of-a-kind wearable art garments. She is active in church work and local sewing and quilting clubs. Kelly lives in Florence, Kentucky.

SHAPED-UP SWEATSHIRT

The designer of the Shaped-Up Sweatshirt retired in 1989 from engineering management in the communications industry to be an at-home mom. **Steph Barry** reports, "Being at home has given me time to rediscover sewing and the creative outlet it can provide." She lives in Grayslake, Illinois, with her husband, Jim, and sons, Michael and Kevin.

Bibliography

Betzina Webster, Sandra. *More Power Sewing.* New York, N.Y.: Practicality Press, 1993.

Grayson, Beatriz M. "Easy Appliqué for Complex Shapes." Threads (August/September 1995), p. 69.

Mulari, Mary. *Accents for Your Style.* Aurora, Minn.: Mary's Productions, 1990.

———. *Mary Mulari's Garments with Style,* Radnor, Pa.: Chilton Book Company, 1995.

———. *Minnesota Applique Designs.* Aurora, Minn.: Mary's Productions, 1985.

———. *Sweatshirts with Style.* Radnor, Pa.: Chilton Book Company, 1993.

Saunders, Jan. *Jan Saunders' Wardrobe Quick-Fixes.* Radnor, Pa.: Chilton Book Company, 1995.

Index

♦ Applique
    "bra syndrome" and, 4
    dimensional, 75–78
    on mittens, 111–114
    satin stitch, 73–74
    scissor cuttings, 81–83
    scrub stitch, 79–80

♦ Banded Cardigan with Contrast Ribbing, 52–55
Banded Cardigan with Matching Ribbing, 48–51
Barry, Steph, 136–140, 149
Bednar, Nancy, 119–121, 148
Books, resource, 146
"Bra syndrome," 4
Buttons
    funnel collar with, 23–24
        shoulder opening and, 24–27
Buttons and Bows Sweatshirt, 116–118

♦ Cardigans
    banded
        with contrast ribbing, 52–55
        with matching ribbing, 48–51
    mock front, with dickey insert, 87–89
    zip-front, 43–47
Caring for sweatshirts, 3–4
Casing, elastic, 72
Center front line on sweatshirt, 5
Chalk marker, 3

Circle Neckline with Fabric Insert, 40–42
Circle Neckline with Running Stitches, 38–39
Closures, 115. *See also specific types*
Collars. *See also* Necklines
    cross-over ribbing, 17–19
    funnel
        with buttons, 23–24
        with buttons and shoulder opening, 24–27
        with drawstring, 27–29
        with woven (non-stretch) fabric, 29–31
        with zipper, 21–22
    mock front and large, 84–86
    neckline, 31–32
    new seam for, in neckline, 9
    overlapping, 20
    polo
        in large-collar mock front, 84–86
        two-piece, 31–32
        two-polo, 20
    understitching new, 10–11
    zipper, 13–16
Cool and Unusual Stripes, 105–107
Cord bunches, 115
Cross-Over Ribbing Collar, 17–19
Cuffs
    facings for, 10
    replacement sleeve, 56–57
    two-piece, 57–58

♦ Darts, 72
Decoration. *See* Applique; Embellishments
Dickey
    mock front cardigan with insert of, 87–89
    neckline with, 36–37
Dimensional Applique with Tulle, 75–78
Drawstrings, 27–29, 72

♦ Easy-Lace Buttonhole Trim, 96–98
Edges
    checking/fixing bottom, 12
    facings for, 10
    non-fray, 99–101
Elastic casing, 72
Elegant Beaded Sweatershirt, 119–121
Embellishments. *See also* Applique
    "bra syndrome" and, 4
    easy-lace buttonhole trim, 96–98
    fleece-woven front, 99–101
    large-collar mock front, 84–86
    mock front cardigan with dickey insert, 87–89
    mock front placket with toggle closure, 90–92
    Nordic sweatshirt, 93–95
    relaxed weaving, 102–104
    sponge painting and stitching, 108–110
    stripes, unusual, 105–107
    zippered sleeve pockets, 61–63

Equipment for working with sweatshirts, 2–4, 147

▶ Fabric painting, 108–110
Fabrics
    insert, circle neckline with, 40–42
    mail-order resources for, 147
    painting on, 108–110
    prewashing, 3
    supply of, 3
    thread and, 3
    woven (non-stretch), 29–31
Facings
    for cuffs, 10
    for edges, 10
    hem, with shirttails, 64–65
    for necklines, 9–10
Flatlock Frenzy, 122–124
Fleece-Woven Front, 99–101
From the Wilds of Canada, 141–145
Funnel Collar and Shoulder Opening, 24–27
Funnel Collar with Buttons, 23–24
Funnel Collar with Woven (non-stretch) Fabric, 29–31
Funnel Collar with Zipper, 21–22
Funnel Drawstring Collar, 27–29

▶ Gatz, Marilyn, 116–118, 148
Giblin, Janis, 125–126, 149

▶ Harlow, Kelly, 127–129, 149
Hem Facing with Shirttails, 64–65

Hems
    tunic extension with zipper, 66–68
    two-piece tunic extension, 68–70
    wide, fixing, 72
Hidden Side Pocket with Triangle Ends, 70–71

▶ Interfacing, 3
Iron, 2

▶ Labels, instructional, 3–4
Lacing, 72
Large-Collar Mock Front, 84–86
Life's a Party Sweatshirt, 127–129

▶ Mail-order resources, 147
Marking pens, washable, 3
Mitten Gallery, 111–114
Mock Front Cardigan with Dickey Insert, 87–89
Mock front, large-collar, 84–86
Mock Front Placket with Toggle Closures, 90–92
Mulari, Mary, 1, 150

▶ Necklines. *See also* Collars; *specific projects*
    circle
        with fabric insert, 40–42
        with running stitches, 38–39
    collar, 31–32
    with dickey, 36–37

facings for, 9–10
marking quarter portions of, 8–9
measuring around, with tape measure, 6
new collar seam in, positioning, 9
overlapping, 20
seam allowance for, covering, 11
staystitching, before removing ribbing, 6–7
understitching new, 10–11
U, with insert, 33–35
Nordic Sweatshirt, 93–95

▶ Osborn, Jenny, 122–124, 148
Overlapping neckline, 20

▶ Paper-backed fusible web, 3
Placket, mock front, 90–92
Pockets
    hidden side, with triangle ends, 70–71
    zipper sleeve, 61–63
Polo collars
    in large-collar mock front, 84–86
    two, 20
    two-piece, 31–32
Prihoda, Barb, 130–135, 149

▶ Relaxed Weaving, 102–104
Replacement Sleeve Cuffs, 56–57
Resources
    books, 146
    mail-order, 147

Ribbing

contrasting effect with, 17–19, 52–55

crossover collar and, 17–19

matching effect with, 48–51

removing, 7–8

saving, 8

staystitching neckline before removing, 6–7

Running stitches

in applique mittens, 111–114

circle neckline with, 38–40

▶ Satin stitch applique, 73–74

Saunders, Jan, 141–145, 149

Scandinavian-style sweatshirt, 93–95

Scherenschnitte, 81–83

Scissor Cuttings Applique, 81–83

Scrub Stitch Applique, 79–80

Serger, 2

Sewing machine, 2–3

Shaped-Up Sweatshirt, 136–140

Sleeve-Gathering Trim, 59–60

Sleeves, shortening, 59–60

Some Bunny Sweatshirt, 125–126

Sponge Painting and Stitching, 108–110

Stabilizers, 3

Staystitching, 6–7

Stripes, unusual, 105–107

Supplies for working with sweatshirts, 2–4, 147

Sweatshirts. *See also specific parts of; specific projects*; Techniques for working with sweatshirts

caring for, 3–4

center front line on, 5

equipment for working with, 2–4, 147

fit of, 4–5

labels for, instructional, 3–4

prewashing, 3

supplies for working with, 2–4, 147

supply of, 3

trying on, 4–5

▶ Tape measure, 3, 6

Techniques for working with sweatshirts. *See also specific techniques*

adding zipper with hidden seams, 11–12

checking/fixing sweatshirt bottom edge after removing ribbing, 12

covering back neck seam allowances, 11

making facings, 9–10

marking quarter portions of necklines, 8–9

measuring around neckline with tape measure, 6

positioning new collar seam in necklines, 9

removing ribbing, 7–8

staystitching neckline before removing ribbing, 6–7

understitching new necklines or collars, 10–11

Thread, 3, 115

Toggle closures, 90–92

Trims

easy-lace buttonhole, 96–98

ideas for, 115

sleeve-gathering, 59–60

Trio of Trillium sweatshirt, 130–135

Tulle, dimensional applique with, 75–78

Tunic Extension with Zipper, 66–68

Two-Piece Cuffs, 57–58

Two-Piece Polo Collar, 31–32

Two-Piece Tunic Extension, 68–70

Two-Polo Collar Overlapping Neckline, 20

▶ Understitching, 10–11

U Neck with Insert, 33–35

▶ Weaving

fleece-woven front, 99–101

relaxed, 102–104

▶ Yoke, front, 93–95

▶ Zip-Front Cardigan, 43–47

Zipper Collar, 13–16

Zippered Sleeve Pockets, 61–63

Zippers

on cardigan front, 43–47

collar, 13–16

funnel collar with, 21–22

with hidden seams, adding, 11–12

in sleeve pockets, 61–63

tunic extension with, 66–68

About the Author

Mary Mulari has been teaching and writing about creative sewing techniques since 1982, when she began offering "Designer Sweatshirts" classes through the local community education program. From her home base in Aurora, Minnesota, she has written ten books and contributed articles to *Woman's World, Workbasket, Sewing Update Newsletter* and the American Sewing Guild's newsletter, *Notions*. She continues to travel to present seminars around the U.S. and in Canada and to collect ideas for new books and sewing projects. She has designed patterns for the McCall Pattern Company and has been featured as a guest on sewing television programs, including frequent appearances on "Sewing with Nancy." In her non-sewing life, Mary volunteers for community events such as the annual Pumpkin Fest quilt show and the Holiday Heritage Festival in December for which she designs the special postal cancellation stamp and sews a raffle prize: a designer sweatshirt. She enjoys reading, chocolate, and meeting and hearing from her students and readers of her books. You are welcome to write to her at Mary's Productions, Box 87-C3, Aurora, MN 55705.

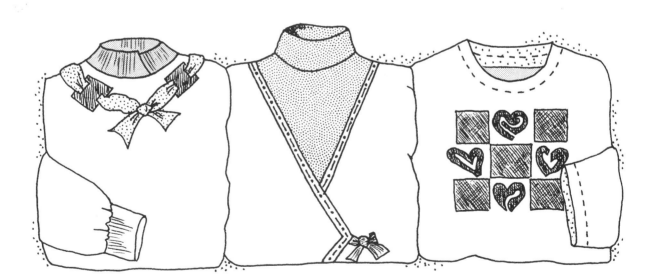